7/30/99

To: Vickie,

When you finish reading
this you'll hesitate
to feed the gulls.

Mark A. Farris

Published by Software Et Cetera
Norristown, PA

Copyright © 1994 by Mark A. Davis

ISBN 0-9652627-0-7

Publisher's note: This is a work of fiction. The characters, incidents, and
dialogues are products of the author's imagination and are not to be con-
strued as real. Where the names of actual persons, living or dead, are used,
the situations, incidents, and dialogues concerning those persons are
entirely fictional and are not intended to depict any actual events or
change the entirely fictional nature of the work.

Manufactured in the United States of America.

First Edition 1996

I suppose we all have fed the sea gulls at one time or another. Each passing minute we try to bring them closer to us. The challenge to get them to take the food from our fingers both excites, delights, yet scares us. I've watched them land on the sand and stalk beach goers for tiny morsels of food. Like carefree mavericks of the sky they soar overhead, land and gather around us. How strange these fanciful birds of the sky can be - untamed since the dawn of time. If we respect their fragile world they will remain unhindered until eternity. This book is a tribute to the ballet of the gulls, the beauty of the beach and the wonder of imagination. May they fly away - laughing.

Meanwhile, here on earth, I would like to thank some very special people who have helped me on this journey. Thank you to my parents who took me to Brigantine Island as a small boy and allowed me to feed the gulls and experience the wonders of the beach and ocean. Thanks to my brother Barry and his wife Julie, who provided me with the computer to facilitate these words. Thanks to my sisters, Lynda and Kathy, who were my editors, each helped me to control my run-on sentences. To my very dear friends, Ron and Reneé Martin who shared their graphics expertise, endless hours of help, and unbending faith in this project. May we all spend more time - laughing.

Dedicated to:
Jacque Jett
My eternal flame of optimism

GULLS
By: Mark A. Davis

The Reflection

It was predictable that the temperature would suddenly change on the day after Labor Day. This year was no exception. The early morning sunlight helped to make the Kansas air a little warmer, but the chilly breeze swept across the cornfield and buffeted against the home of Marina and David Spencer.

Marina stood on her patio with a cup of tea resting in the palm of her left hand. She was glad that the summer was finally over. As she watched the swallows dart and dive in playful chase over the fields behind her house, she kept thinking of how glad she was to have returned to Kansas, and to the safety of her home in the middle of a two hundred acre cornfield.

Her husband David, built the house for her and the children, and they were proud of it. The design was for the most part, theirs. The exterior was a typical Williamsburg Colonial, but David added the features that were necessary to withstand the cold Kansas winters.

Marina and David, had planned a large family, but after having their second child, Christopher, they found out that they could not have any more children. The childbirth of Chris was very difficult. So, unless they were to adopt at some point, the house with five bedrooms, each having a full bath, was just a little more than they would need.

Marina had looked forward to the vacation in the east and would have even considered moving to the coast. However, the vacation had turned into her worst nightmare, and she realized afterward that she would never leave Kansas again.

CHAPTER ONE:

The Rutledge Place

Erica and Christopher meant everything in the world to Marina. Erica was eleven, and Chris was nine. They both had birthdays on exactly the same day - August thirty-first. Marina and David decided this year that they would all go away for vacation, something that they had never done before. The computer software business kept David at work for an average of sixty hours a week. The house had taken all of his extra time. Vacations away from the cornfield of Kansas, were out of the question.

Marina was outside, leaning against the sliding glass door, gazing out over the cornfield and thinking of the vacation that had just ended. She could feel the coldness of the glass against her back. She didn't know if it was the cold that caused her to have goose bumps appear on her arms, or if it was the thought of the recent trip. She took a sip of her hot tea and, as the swallows chirped and chased each other, Marina tried to calm herself and rid her mind of the weeks past. But she kept thinking of the sea gulls. They kept flashing back in her mind. She was sure that she would never look at them in the same way again. The gulls would never be those beautiful and romantic birds of summer. Suddenly, in a flashback from the beach, Marina gasped, and the cup and saucer fell to the concrete shattering into a hundred pieces.

The name Marina, was given to her by her father. He loved the sea. Both of her parents had died in a fatal lake boating accident when she was two years old. She was sent to Kansas to live with her aunt immediately after the funeral. Marina had no other family, and when her Aunt died, Marina stayed in Kansas. After finishing school, she met David. They had a short courtship then married within six months. Erica came along the very next year. Although Marina's name was very unusual, she enjoyed explaining how her father loved the name and the meaning. Her aunt would tell her over and over why he gave it to her and that it always reminded him of the sea.

David Spencer was born in Brigantine, New Jersey, a small island just off the coast of Atlantic City. He went through school on the island. After college at Temple University and a computer school in Pennsylvania, David returned to Brigantine. The computer industry, however, sent him to Phoenix, Arizona, and then, eventually, to a company office in Kansas City, Kansas.

For years, he told Marina of the beauty of the island

and the beauty of the ocean. She had never been to the coast and had never seen a large body of water, least of all, the sea. From time to time, she would ask David if he missed life on the island, and asked him if he wished to return.

His answer would always be the same. Someday, maybe, they would go on vacation to the island and he would show them the magnificent Atlantic Ocean, where the ocean breeze cools the summer and the sea gulls soar and circle over the golden beaches.

The phone call came in June from David's friend in Brigantine, New Jersey. They were best friends when they were in high school, but they had gone their separate directions once they were involved in their careers. Mark had always wanted David to come to the island again for a visit, but David could never seem to find the time. This time, however, would be different.

David was being sent to Atlantic City for a computer conference that would last for a week. After that week, he planned to take the much-needed vacation and he would stay for the additional time in Brigantine. Mark, however, was traveling to England on business and would be gone the entire time that David was in New Jersey. It was Mark's suggestion that they stay in his house while he was gone. The house was right on the beach at the south end of the island. He had the place built to his strict specifications and he left very little out of the plans.

The house was almost five thousand square feet. Two sides were almost all glass. People walking the beach would stop in front of the house and stare at the magnificent contemporary mansion. The home had been featured in Architectural Digest magazine, and also had a few seconds on "Lifestyles of the Rich and Famous". Mark acquired most of his money from the stock market and managed to escape the stock disaster of 1989. He somehow profited from the experience, and now had a most impressive portfolio. So impressive, in fact, that he didn't seem to work much at all. Instead, he would use his self employed company name as an excuse to travel the world.

The invitation to stay at Mark's home in New Jersey seemed to be the right offer at the right time. David, could take the family to Brigantine, and they would stay on the beach. David took the savings that he had for their lodging, and gave it to Marina to spend on clothes for herself and the children. The air-fare for all of them would be expensive, and the cost of having someone take care of their home in Kansas would add to the expense. They also had to put the two golden retrievers in the kennel for the time they would be away. But, the vacation would still be relatively cheap, thanks to Mark and his offer.

Marina began shopping right away for the items that she would need for the vacation. She and her girl friend Karen, made routine trips to the shopping mall. In the beginning of summer, the mall almost acted as babysitter for the children. She and Karen could shop while their kids would go to a movie, or just " hang out. "

David didn't get too much involved with the planning and the packing for the trip. During his long hours at the office, he occasionally thought of how nice it would be to have a vacation with his family. He promised Marina that this would truly be the best vacation she ever had. He also promised her that she wouldn't have to cook or to do a thing. Mark arranged for his housekeeper to stay with them, and she would take care of all their needs. David agreed to pay her small salary. She would stay at the house for the entire time, not only as a housekeeper, but as a baby sitter . They would only have to enjoy the beaches and the night life.

Since David had left the area, many casinos had been built in Atlantic City, changing the skyline drastically from what David remembered. The old famous hotels were demolished and the new towering casino hotels were built almost overnight. This made Atlantic City one of the hot spots on the east coast for entertainment.

Brigantine, New Jersey, was a residential island, six miles long and three miles wide. The casino hotels of Atlantic City, however, had caused the sudden encroachment of new homes to be built on the island, which was directly off the coast from the city. In the last three years, the land developers from the mainland had filled in an additional two thousand acres of swamp land and had built an additional one thousand homes. The once-quiet residential island had now become the residential "place to be". Any of the older small single family summer vacation homes were being renovated to accommodate the influx of casino employees looking for a place to live. Thousands of hotel and casino workers began moving into efficiency apartments, that were quickly becoming available to them. There were many long-time residents of the island who were seeking the fast casino dollar.

All of this was still to be a surprise to David and his family. Mark's house, however, was protected from the encroachment of neighbors. He had bought many acres of land, and could afford to protect himself from the new island development. He also had enough money stashed away in investments that he would never have to sell any of his high priced land. He bought the plans for the contemporary house from a friend in Virginia. Mark was so pleased with the design and the size of the home, that he named the house after the house he so loved in Virginia. On the beach in front of the mansion, he had erected an expensive gold leaf sign with the words "Rutledge Place". The address was so impressive that mail would be received if only addressed   " Rutledge Place, Brigantine, NJ."

Marina was very organized in everything that she did. Packing for the vacation meant that she would make lists of everything that they would need. Packing for the beach, however, was something that she had never done before, so she had to solicit help from Karen. Karen had been to the beach in Florida many times and was very able in giving Marina some helpful hints.

While Marina was packing one of seven suitcases,

the television was on in the bedroom. One of those afternoon talk shows became little more than back-ground noise, as Marina neatly folded her clothes.

" Be on the lookout, for the dark, long-haired fox !" the announcer said.

Marina turned to look at the TV screen because the phrase had caught her attention. It was obviously a commercial. The picture was a young girl walking the beach. She had what would be considered the perfect shape and the perfect body motion for a very revealing thong bathing suit that showed most of her rear end.

"... for she is soon becoming an endangered species," the announcer continued.

The girl was holding something in her right hand. A quick series of edits eventually revealed the product. "Olana Sun Screen", the announcer said.

" Don't you... become one of the endangered species. Protect your skin. Use Olana Sun Screen."

The camera backed away, showing the ocean and hundreds of people lying on the beach, getting sun-tanned.

" For without the use of protective sun-screen, you ... could become the true endangered species." the commercial ended.

Marina watched for a second, looking forward to the time that she would spend on the beach as the programming returned to the talk show. Karen had heard enough and decided to turn off the television and listen to the stereo instead.

The flight to Philadelphia and start of the vacation would begin tomorrow. Marina had all of the suitcases open on the bed and around the room. She methodically checked off each item from her list. Tonight, she would have to go out again and get some of the last minute items. A supply of toothpaste and shampoo for the children, and the complement of aspirin and suntan lotion that they would be needing. Karen told her to be sure to get those supplies before she left. The stores at the beach were known to jack up the prices of those items when they knew they had a captive audience. So Karen made sure that she had all the supplies purchased and packed in Kansas.

In the morning, David took the dogs to the kennel. The children went with him in their minivan, which gave Marina the additional time she needed to double check all of the items. By the time they returned, she had everything packed, the suitcases closed, and the house ready for their departure. When David pulled into the driveway, the boy who lived on the farm down the road was just leaving. Marina had paid him some money in advance for cutting the lawn while they would be gone. He would also check on the house each day, and take in the newspapers and mail. The Spencer's had known the boy for many years and felt that he was very responsible and reliable. As he turned the van into the driveway, the boy gave him a quick wave from his bicycle and continued down the long road to his farmhouse

Erica ran from the van into the house, yelling to her mother, " Don't forget the popcorn! I need it to feed the gulls on the beach!"

" I didn't, dear, don't worry," Marina replied.

For the last three weeks, all Erica could talk about was how she planned to feed the sea gulls.

" Ya know, they come from all over to get the popcorn. Sharon told me that if you have enough popcorn, you can have every sea gull in the world right in front of you. They will even eat right from your hand. Isn't that right, Dad?" Erica quizzed in excitement.

" I don't know about right from your hand, dear, but they will come from all along the beach when they see that there's something being handed out."

David started up the stairs to get the suitcases that Marina had set at the top of the steps. Chris was eager to help, getting a small suitcase from inside the bedroom. They had talked every night at dinner about the vacation, and Chris thought that this day would never get here. It was almost like the anticipation of Christmas morning for him. David had promised to take him fishing and water skiing.

It didn't take long to pack the van and check the house over one last time. Soon they were on their way to the airport.

" Do we get to have lunch on the airplane?" Chris asked with excitement.

" I think so," Marina answered.

" I know we get peanuts on the plane," Erica added. " I heard that on TV. They always say something about getting peanuts on the plane."

Erica got excited about anything and everything. Every day was the best adventure to her, and she always made the best of any situation. Even from the time that she was very young, she was happy being alone, for hours and hours, with the simplest and the smallest things.

Chris, on the other hand, would have to be constantly amused. He would get bored very quickly and then begin whining. Sometimes, it was almost more than Marina could bear. She made sure that she had a few surprises for Chris. Marina bought a GameBoy at the mall for him. She hoped that she could wait until much later in the trip before she would have to bribe him. The ride to the airport was just filled with the hundreds of questions about the island.

" Do they have wild animals?" he asked his father.

" No , nothing like that. This is a residential island."

" What does residential mean?" Chris quickly asked.

" Well, it means that there are just houses and a beach. And, of course, restaurants and a few small motels. But, for the most part, Chris, there are just houses on the island. There is one half of the island that is a bird sanctuary."

" What's a bird sanktary?" Chris was quick to ask.

" A bird sanctuary, dummy," his sister corrected him, laughing "you can't even talk right."

" That is where they have set aside land that you are not allowed to use for anything. You can't build houses, stores or anything like that," his mother said.

" You're not even allowed to go swimming on that part of the island," David said.

" I can remember when we were kids, we used to sneak down to the reservation, the bird sanctuary, and rip off our clothes and go skinny dipping," David said, glancing at Marina.

" Then, the beach patrol would spot us with their binoculars, turn on the flashing lights, and try to catch us. We were damned good at out-running them. We would run across the sand up over the sand dunes. They could never find us. Eventually, they would give up, and then we would go back into the water buck naked again," he said.

The afternoon sun was warm, coming through the windows of the van, and David had to turn the air conditioner on high just to keep it at a comfortable temperature. The remainder of the ride to the airport was uneventful. The children continued to ask all sorts of questions about the island and the beach, and they even found themselves repeating some of the same questions. Soon, they came to the off ramp to the airport. Chris loved watching the huge airliners that came low over the highway on their approach to the runway.

David turned the van into the parking lot that was marked by the large blue sign " Long Term Parking". On business trips, he had to leave the car at the airport for weeks at a time. He had his favorite spot at the far end of the parking lot, and he used to instinctively park the car in the same place, not even looking up at the sign marking what section of the airport lot he was in. Once he had returned to the airport, only to find that he had parked his car at the other end of the lot. Not looking at the sign when he left, meant that when he returned, he could not find the car. He walked the lot for more than a hour before he finally found it.

Marina made a mental note of the area of the parking lot that they had parked, but didn't mention it to David. Instead, when she got into the terminal, she wrote the letter "C-3" on a slip of paper and placed it in her wallet.

To the children this was the trip of a lifetime. They had never been on an airplane, and they had never been to the beach. For them, the wait inside the terminal for the plane boarding call seemed to take forever. Chris would try to escape from his mother's view to check out the rest of the terminal. He was not at all afraid of losing them. Even at his young age, he knew that they were not about to leave without him. Therefore, he could explore and not have to worry. Marina repeatedly asked that he stay put. Nothing seemed to work though. As soon as her head was turned, he was off again.

The trip was non-stop to Philadelphia, but it would take them more than three hours. There was a movie to watch on the plane, which Marina hoped would keep the kids busy for a time. If, it was a movie that would hold their interest. Marina wasn't much on waiting in airports. She felt that they actually left the house too early. David sat reading a novel about the space shuttle. Once he started reading something, the world could almost come to an end and crumble around him before he would notice.

" Erica, would you please find your brother and bring him back here?" Marina asked in a firm voice.

" He'll be back before we go. Do I have to?" she pleaded.

" American flight seven one seven, non stop service

to Philadelphia, will be boarding at gate twenty one," the woman's voice stated over the PA system.

" I'll get him," David responded to Marina.

It wasn't long before he returned to the rows of red chairs at the gate, when the woman on the loud-speaker said," American flight seven one seven, non-stop service for Philadelphia is now boarding.

All at once, everyone in the waiting area began gathering their belongings and started for the tele-scope ramp that led to the airliner. The woman in a navy blue pin striped suit stood at the doorway and checked each boarding pass before letting the pas-sengers continue down the ramp to the door of the airplane.

" How are you young man?" she asked, as Chris and Erica got to her.

David handed the woman all four of the boarding slips and they were allowed to pass. Chris started run-ning down the ramp to the airplane but was abruptly stopped by the stewardess at the entrance. He slipped past her while she was looking at the boarding passes and stood looking at the flight deck and the crew.

"Wow!" he exclaimed, as he watched the flight crew checking switches in the overhead panels.

Inside the cockpit, the crew was going through the pre-flight list, and dialing in the required radio fre-quencies for the flight. To the novice, this seemed like an endless series of complicated maneuvers. Yet, it was just routine, that seemed to take a half an hour or more. While the passengers were getting situated in the cabin, the stewardesses were busy helping the passengers stow away their small bags in the overhead compartments. You could easily tell the business travelers. They were the ones that knew how large the overhead compartments were. They didn't take more than a second to throw their bags in the overhead compartment and then flop into the seat below. The newer passengers were the ones that required the help of the steward or stewardess in putting their things away. The stewardess made the ritual journey from the front of the plane to the back, checking to make sure that all the passengers had their seat belts on and that there wasn't anything on the floor that should be in the overhead compartment.

The airplane at that point began to get very warm. The temperature outside was nearing eighty degrees, and the temperature inside seemed to be nearing one hundred. There was a mixture of perfumes and cologne that filled the air. It also was very crowded. The plane was, of course, over-booked for the flight. The next step was the stewardess asking if anyone would be willing to give up their seat, for a first class seat on another flight at a later time. This was becoming a ritual for the airlines. They always over-booked the flight and then would have to nearly beg people to trade tickets. This seemed to be a unique way to make sure that the plane left the terminal with all the seats full, and also to get some people on the flights that would normally leave half-empty.

Marina and David sat on the aisle seats and left the window seats for the two kids. Chris sat with his face pressed to the window. Marina thought that's where he might stay for the entire trip. Erica fumbled through the in-flight magazines that were located in the seat back, while she waited patiently.

Shortly, the doors to the 757 jetliner were closed, and the airplane was pushed from the terminal building. Everyone on board seemed to have something to do. David continued to read the novel and didn't have much to say. Marina watched the other passengers and occasionally answered another one of Erica's many questions.

" On behalf of Captain Barnes and the rest of the flight crew of American flight seven, one, seven, I would like to welcome you on board American's non-stop service to Philadelphia," the stewardess said over the loudspeaker system.

Outside the 757 jetliner, the airport area was getting much busier. Three airliners were pushed from the ramp at exactly the same time, and all would soon be heading down the long taxi-way to the main runway. Four airplanes were on their way to the terminal from the runway. Within the next half hour, the international airport would be saturated with people and planes during this busiest time of day.

Chris didn't take his face away from the window for a second. He didn't even ask any questions. He just marveled at the activity and at the sounds of the huge jets that took off past them as their plane continued down the taxi-way.

The jet sat at the end of the runway for a few minutes, and then everyone inside could hear the jet engines come alive. It wasn't long before the huge 757 began the turn for the center line of the main runway. Chris turned his head for just a second to look at his mother and then, as the inside cabin lights blinked on and off, he returned to the window. Erica was pushed against the seat as the airplane began the race to the airspeed necessary to become airborne. After some bumps from the runway below, and some yawing of the tail of the airplane, it lifted from the concrete and into a steep climb, straight out from the runway. Within seconds, the landing gear was retracted, and the plane became streamlined and more than fit for the high altitude climb.

David never stopped reading, and Marina wasn't even sure he knew that they had, in fact, left the ground. After a few bounces they experienced as they flew through the cold air inside the clouds, the airliner settled into a two thousand five hundred feet per minute climb, to a flight level of thirty seven thousand feet. There they would stay, for nearly three hours, until they would begin the descent to the Philadelphia International Airport.

Summer heat meant that the upper level air would be unstable. The afternoon thunderstorms had already developed and were moving slowly eastward. The line of storms stretched from the Great Lakes to as far south as the Tennessee valley. The airliner cruised along at thirty seven thousand feet. Now, they were flying many thousand feet above the tops of the cumulus clouds, and the thunderstorms below. The passengers aboard the flight experienced an occasional series of bumps as the jet skipped across the unstable air.

Marina worried about each and every ripple in the air. Every time the airliner bounced, she would look up from the magazine that she was reading and look toward the front of the plane in concern.

" Ladies and gentleman, we may experience some unstable air up here today," the pilot stated over the loudspeaker system." For your safety and comfort, we would like you to remain in your seats and keep your seat belts securely fastened."

David assured Marina that this was routine and the pilots always make that statement, even with the slightest ripple of unstable air.

Christopher still had his head against the window trying to see anything that he could. At the high altitude, with the bright white tops of the clouds below, he had little more to see. But the ever-changing view of snow white clouds kept his attention. Also, the excitement of flying was enough to keep him fascinated.

The remainder of the flight to Philadelphia was calm and fast. It wasn't long before the jet engine noise all but stopped, and the people felt as though they were sitting in an airplane that wasn't even moving. The noise and the motion just seemed to stop as the airliner began to slow and begin the decent.

Suddenly, the jet splashed through some clouds, and the people were jolted from their almost sleeping state. All at once, the passengers began talking with each other.

"Ladies and Gentlemen, we are beginning our descent to Philadelphia. We should be on the ground at the airport in about ten minutes," the Captain stated.

GULLS

The stewardesses made a last sweep of the cabin with their plastic bags opened, collecting trash from the passengers. Soon, the sound of the engines increased, and the jet began a hard bank to the left. David watched out the window as the jet descended through the clouds, then burst out from the clouds into the cooler air below. The city of Philadelphia could be seen about fifteen miles away. The grey-blue mammoth skyscrapers reached out of the Pennsylvania landscape below and looked like jetties of ancient carved rocks protruding into the afternoon sky. A wide and winding river divided the city from the lush green of the Fairmount Park, and the blanket of row houses to the south and west of the city.

As the jet turned on the final approach to the airport, the city disappeared under the rear wing. It seemed to take forever it to get close to the runway. As it dropped lower and lower to the ground, the sound of the engines increased. Some of the passengers that were not used to flying sat in the seats and showed some concern on their faces because of the noise. As the afternoon thermal air current brushed against the underside of the wings, the airliner would shift from one side to the other. As the passengers rocked back and forth, the pilot increased the power of the engines. An occasional added bounce caused some of the passengers, including Marina and Erica, to worry. The pilot accurately steered the jet to the center line of the runway, and the wheels soon slammed hard against the concrete. The nose wheel followed shortly and the 757 was safely on the runway, and rolling along the hot surface. The passengers were all leaning forward, as the reverse thrust and the braking of the jet liner slowed the huge vehicle to a crawl.

Without delay, the businessmen raised from their seats and began removing their briefcases and small bags from the overhead compartment. While the stewardess was announcing their arrival and asking that the passengers please remain in their seats, people were already starting to walk forward to the door paying little regard to her plea.

Chris and Erica were more than an little excited about their arrival, and like the businessmen that were already filling the aisles, they too, wanted to get off the plane.

It was now almost six o'clock in the evening. The terminal of the airport was at near capacity. This was without a doubt the busiest time of the day for the airport.

" I'm very surprised that we arrived on time," David told Marina. " Usually at this time of day, the airlines are backed up and everything coming or going is late."

The airport had been renovated since the last time that David Spencer was there. The task of getting luggage was made a lot easier. By the time they took the walk down the concourse and the escalator to the baggage claim area, the bags would be traveling around the carousel, waiting for them. As usual, the bags did not arrive in a group. The first three of the seven bags arrived together, but the remaining four, seemed to take forever to make the appearance on the carousel. All in all, the entire process was somewhat orderly, much to David's surprise. He removed all the luggage from the carousel, with the help of Erica and Chris, who were pointing and yelling every time they would see another bag burst through from the other side of the wall.

David arranged for the rental car company to have a convertible waiting for them. He thought that a convertible would make for much more fun for the vacation. They had planned to see a lot while they were at Brigantine. The island was only less than an hour from the city of Philadelphia, which meant that they could visit some of the historic areas, Independence Hall, Valley Forge, Philadelphia Zoo, Philadelphia Museum of Art, etc.

David knew that they would have to have a good dinner before they could start out from the city and head to the beach. He had always promised Marina that he would take her to one of the older restaurants in the city. This would be a good time. Bookbinders Restaurant, was perhaps one of the oldest in the city and had atmosphere that would impress Marina. From the airport, he called ahead for reservations. Much to his surprise, they were able to accommodate the four of them. The ride from the airport was exciting for the children, especially when David made a wrong turn and ended up in the center of the city. Erica couldn't believe how tall the buildings were and commented that she felt that they were falling. She rested her head on the back of the seat in the convertible and stared straight up at the sky as her father drove through the city to the south side. The feeling was exhilarating to her.

Erica and Chris finished their dinner quickly, and waited for Marina and David to have two cups of coffee each. Soon after, they were on their way. By this time, the sun was already setting. As they approached the off ramp of the Atlantic City Expressway, they could see the skyline of Atlantic City sprawled across the horizon to the east. Each of the hotels had arranged spotlights so that the buildings were brightly lit. Atlantic City appeared to be trying to beat Las Vegas with the number of lights they could use on the buildings. Without exaggeration, there appeared to be more than a million lights on just one casino. The buildings' lights, as seen from a distance, sparkled like a strand of jewels against the night sky. The skyline stretched along the coast for four miles. The air blowing in the convertible was warm. The thunderstorms that they had flown over, on their way into Philadelphia, had never made it to the coast. Instead, they dissipated, leaving the evening sky clear of clouds. The first stars were beginning to appear, and the sky to the west had an overwhelming display of mauve, deep violet and blue-green. Marina felt that it was all very romantic. She couldn't wait until she and David could spend some quality time just walking along the beach and watching the sunset.

David pulled the car up to the stop sign and waited for the long lines of traffic to clear. Directly in front of them, was the "Trump Castle Casino-Hotel". The large letters "Trump Castle" stretched from the ground

GULLS

floor of the hotel up to the sixth floor. The huge spot-lights that were aimed onto the walls of the hotel illuminated the entire side of the building. The light escaped from the top edge of the building and continued up into the evening sky. Hundreds of sea gulls swirled around over the hotel catching the many bugs that were attracted by the bright lights. Erica was the first to notice them.

" Mom, look at all those birds up there !" she yelled.

Marina and the kids gazed up at the dark sky over the hotel. The underside of the gulls wings illuminated against the night sky making them look even more predominant than they would normally. An occasional gull would dive to the center of the lights and catch a moth from the air. The gulls criss-crossed each other continually, coming within inches of each other, yet never colliding. While David waited for the opening in the evening traffic, the kids watched the gulls and their feeding frenzy over the hotel.

The bridge from Atlantic City to Brigantine Island was a half-mile long. Fluorescent lights lined the sides of the bridge and the top edge of the railing preventing the family from seeing the ocean off to the right side of the bridge. All they could see was the darkness of night past the rail. Suddenly, a gull came to the top of the rail and flew along with the car. It flew with them for some time, then quickly vanished over the rail and down to the water beneath the bridge.

When they reached the center of the bridge they could see Brigantine Island in front of them. At the entrance to the island, there was a lighthouse which was now used as a library. It was built in 1924 as an advertising promotion to lure people to the island and to sell them property. This smaller than usual lighthouse, was the focal point and symbol of Brigantine Island. The recent renovation of it included the addition of a working light in the circular room at the top, which had been taken from a ship's light. The ship lights that had been used for years as markers had been retired and replaced by high-tech lights. After years of fund raising, the islanders were finally able to have the lighthouse restored to its original condition. The light now rotated and beamed a steady ray of light over the island and out to sea.

Chris and Erica couldn't wait for the break of day tomorrow and to get to the beach. Although David and Marina had a lot to do to get them settled into "Rutledge Place", they too couldn't wait for their time for relaxation on the beach. For David, relaxation would have to wait. He had to report to the hotel in Atlantic City, early in the morning. The seminar and computer convention would begin promptly at nine o'clock. Marina would have to deal with getting everything in order and getting the children to the beach.

As they turned onto Beach Avenue and headed toward the ocean, they could smell the salt air blowing in from the Atlantic. It smelled good, different, nothing like anything they had ever experienced before, and nothing they would ever forget. Marina felt that this was the perfect time for a vacation. She and David had worked very hard for all that they had, but it was time to enjoy this period of their married life together.

When David turned the car into the gravel drive that led to the contemporary house called "Rutledge Place", all Marina could say was, " Oh my God !".

The house seemed to tower above all the homes that were near it. The front of the house that faced the ocean had a glass wall that was at least thirty feet high. The curtains that hung inside the glass, stretched from the floor of the first level to the ceiling of the third level. The rooms inside didn't touch the front wall. In fact, the levels were suspended on three sides. The master bedroom was hanging from steel cables that were attached to the huge wooden beams in the ceiling. The lights inside the house displayed a warm amber glow that illuminated across the sand to the water's edge. The ocean waves couldn't be seen until they broke against the light, looking like lighted dashes of white that would appear and then disappear. The endless recycling of the ocean water that reached the beach as crashing waves created the lulling sound that was very relaxing to listen to. With the engine of the car quiet, they all sat there, taking it in. To them, it was magnificent - the smell, the sound, and the feel of the gentle ocean breeze. David turned from the front seat and with a smile, said,"We're here !"

CHAPTER TWO:
Waves of Wings

When the eight-foot tall oak door was opened, the Spencer's were met by a short woman with white hair. She appeared to be in her thirties or more. Marina had figured she was forty or maybe a little older.

" Hello, ya must be the Spencer's," she said as she sized them up and down.

"Yes. And you are?" David asked.

" I'm Kathleen, Mark's housekeeper."

" Pleased to meet you. This is my wife, Marina."

David went through the introductions.

" Mr. Wilson said that you would be stayin' until after Labor Day. Is that bein' correct, sir?" she asked as she opened the door all the way.

David liked her strong accent.

" Yes, we're staying through next week and will be leaving on Labor Day, the fifth of September," David added as they entered the foyer.

"Well, sir, you certainly will be likin' it here on the

beach, especially the children."

David placed the accent as Scottish, with maybe some English or Welsh influence. He figured that Marina was sure to find out the life history of Kathleen and share that information with him later. Kathleen led the way down the hall toward the bedrooms at the end.

" The children will be stayin' in here, ma'am."

Kathleen opened the door to the right of the hall, and then opened the door to the room across the hall. Marina liked the fact that the children would be staying on the ground floor and that she and David would have the main bedroom on the upper level. When they returned to the stairs they were led up the stairs to the master bedroom on the second level. The third level was a loft, with a study and a complete library. A large telescope, was focused on a bubble skylight that centered the ceiling over the living room. David estimated that the half-sphere was at least fifteen feet in diameter, and the circle of moonlight peering through the skylight shined an oval directly on the king sized bed.

" And, up here, this'll be your room." Kathleen stated. " I trust this will be okay?"

" Oh, yes," Marina answered. " This will do quite well."

" Then, I'll be seein' you downstairs, later, and I can show you the rest of the house."

The kids stayed with Marina in the master bedroom, until David brought the suitcases from the car then placed them in the hall.

Kathleen met them later in the living room and gave

them a guided tour of the rest of the house. The long curtains that went from the floor of the first level to the ceiling of the loft were operated by electric motor. Kathleen explained that they would automatically close as the afternoon sun demanded. The thermostat controlled the curtains, as well as the air conditioning system and ceiling fans. If there was a rainy day, the curtains would remain open, unless you switched the manual override switch. However, at night, the curtains would automatically close at ten. The lights outside and the indirect lights inside, were also operated by computer and would operate on their own. Even if no one was at home, to the outside world it appeared that there was always someone at home.

Marina was the first to remark about how clean the glass was, and about how much work it must take to keep it clean.

" Yes, ma'am. Mark, I mean Mr. Wilson, ma'am - has a company that comes and does the glass. Each week the glass is cleaned. Usually every Monday, even if it's rainin' ma'am," she told them. " Pays them quite well, he does. So the gentleman doesn't mind at all, even in a storm, rain or shine, the windows are washed."

"Must be nice," Marina said to David as they walked down the hall behind Kathleen.

" Now this'll be the kitchen" she stated. " Don't be afraid to use anythin' you'd like now. Mr. Wilson told me that you are not to worry about a thing. I'll be doin' the marketin' every week. Mark has his special things that I must get."

The remainder of the tour took them through two

additional bedrooms on the main level, a formal dining room and a more casual eating area off the kitchen. Almost every room had a skylight somewhere. The contemporary design allowed for the most creative use of glass. David wondered what the place must be like in a thunderstorm, with all the places for light to blast through. They eventually worked their way back through the family room, which was fully equipped with TV, VCR, stereo and a full-sized billiard table. The living room was by far the most impressive. The floor was made of imported polished Italian marble. The center of the room was covered with the most plush and brilliant sky-blue carpet. In the middle wall of plate glass in the front of the room, there was a sculpture of sea gulls. The art was seven feet tall and almost five feet wide. It was a flock of twelve sea gulls, carved from one piece of wood. Each gull was attached at the wing tip to form the tight grouping.

" Isn't it beautiful?" Kathleen remarked. " It was carved by a blind man. Truly amazin', wouldn't ya say? I can't imagine how he done it, bein' blind and all," she added.

Erica ran her hand over the wing of the gull that was closest to the floor. It had the feel of polished stone she thought, but she could feel every feather. Each was carved in complete detail, right down to the smallest feathers under the birds neck.

" Please, don't touch it," Marina told Erica.

Chris was also about to touch the sculpture when his mother gave him her firm instruction, " Or you either."

The family stood at the window, peering through the glass into the moonlit night, out to the dark and eerie Atlantic Ocean beyond. It was still somewhat early, so there were a few people walking the beach hand in hand.

" Can we go down to the water?" Chris quickly asked.

" No. You will have all the time in the world for that tomorrow," Marina told him. " You better get some sleep tonight so you can spend the day on the beach tomorrow."

The trip must have taken a toll on the Spencers physically because within the hour, they were all sound asleep. Through the night the tide had worked its way closer to the front of the house, and the sounds of the breakers could be heard against the reinforcing wall that ran along the front of the beach house. The ocean, at high tide, was just twenty feet away. Marina woke during the night and lay there for the longest time listening to the ocean sound. She drifted in and out of sleep lulled by the noise of the waves breaking against the wall.

In the morning, they all were awakened by the sound of thunder. The storms that they had flown through on the previous afternoon had finally reached the coast. A cold front was pushing a line of storms and the squalls were forecast to reach the coast by mid-morning. Soon after, they would be pushed out to sea and the rest of the day was forecast to be beautiful. In the meantime, the rain battered the roof of "Rutledge Place".

GULLS

David had to be in Atlantic City by nine o'clock. Kathleen was awake well before dawn and had breakfast prepared for all of them. David stood in the living room with a cup of coffee in his hand, staring at the ocean. He was thinking of how terribly successful Mark must be to have all of this. It made his house and lifestyle in Kansas seem meager. Maybe the computer industry wasn't all that he thought it would be. He had worked long and hard for all that he had, but it would take him another decade or more before he could think of having something this grand.

When Marina entered the room, David had been taking another closer look at the sculpture of the gulls.

" It's something, isn't it?" she said.

" Sure is. This place is magnificent. Mark has done well for himself."

" Yes, David, but it isn't as warm-feeling as our house back in Kansas. I mean, don't you get the feeling that it's just a showcase, and that it really isn't that warm," she said. "Our place feels more like a home than this. You know... more lived-in."

" I guess I see what you mean, but you have to admit... I mean, take a look around. There's not a thing out of place. Everything in this house must have cost him a fortune. A fortune in antiques, a fortune in curtains and lights. A fortune in just the land alone. He must be doing pretty damned well to have all of this," David continued.

" Well look at it this way, David, if it was all that great, why does Mark spend so much time traveling? Hell, I'd stay right here and would be hard pressed to go anywhere if I was him."

David finished his coffee, kissed Marina, and assured her that he wouldn't be too late. He also promised to call from the hotel to see how things were going.

" If you guys are on the beach, Kathleen will tell me."

Suddenly, the heavens opened up, and the rain came down in torrents. Lightning struck out over the water, and they could see the white flash of light spread over the ocean far out to sea, turn to amber and then disappear behind the wall of rain.

" That's if you get out onto the beach today." David added.

Marina walked with him to the door and held the door open slightly as he pulled the raincoat up to the back of his neck and ran to the car. Then she went back upstairs to finish getting their clothes in order.

While she was standing over the bed, removing some of her things from the suitcase, she heard a loud thud against the plate glass. Marina turned toward the sound and saw a sea gull desperately trying to get in. She assumed he was trying to escape the driving rain. Repeatedly, he flew against the glass. Thud. Thud. Thud. It continued screaming and slamming his beak into the wall of glass.

" Go away ! Go away!" Marina called to it.

The gull continued to fly against the window until finally it worked its way to the corner of the building and with help from the wind, was blown out to sea. Marina stood for a minute and watched the gull sway and dive against the strong air currents, fighting to stay airborne above the ocean. That was the first time in her life that she had seen a sea gull up close. Her mind reflected again and again on the screams it was making as it repeatedly slammed itself against the glass. It looked terrified, she thought. She was taken aback by how much expression there was in the gull's face. She could actually see fear in the small round eyes. When the beak was open, she could see its tongue, the red inside of the mouth, and hear the screams even through the thick plate glass. She wondered how many times the birds would injure themselves by slamming against the glass of this house. Marina remembered her aunt telling her when she was a little girl, that when a bird flies into a window - it means that someone will die. Marina never gave it much thought until now, but there was certainly something in the way the gull looked; something about the fear in its eyes; that made her think of the tale.

Erica and Chris ran up the stairs, both yelling. "Mom! Mom! Mom! Are we going to go to the beach today? Will the rain stop, do you think?"

" They say it will," Marina told them. " The weatherman said that the storm will be out to sea later this morning. You can go to the beach later."

Immediately, they both ran back downstairs and to the family room to watch TV a little more.

The rain ended within the hour. By noon, the sky was clear and the ocean looked slate grey, The sensors automatically opened the curtains and the ceiling fans came on low speed. Marina wasn't sure if she liked the idea of the house having a mind of its own, but it did make life easier for controlling the environment and it was comfortable. Erica and Chris didn't realize that the sun was out and the rain had ended. They were so involved in television that they forgot the time. Marina watched the storm clouds moving away; they stopped in a line along the horizon. The afternoon sun highlighted the tops of the cumulus clouds, and she could see the rain still pouring down to the ocean from underneath the storm clouds. But the island was warming rapidly from the strong rays of the sun overhead. Marina thought that, after lunch, the children could go out to the beach with her.

" Can I feed the gulls? Can I?" Erica begged every time she saw her mother.

" After lunch," her mother told her.

At precisely noon Kathleen had lunch ready for them: home-made soup and tomato sandwiches, made from the fresh tomatoes grown in Mark's garden. There was no mistaking the taste and the smell of fresh home grown tomatoes.

After lunch, Erica pleaded once again to go out to the beach to feed the gulls. Kathleen had already made some popcorn for her, and the smell of the freshly popped corn filled the entire house. Chris was willing to wait until Marina was done with unpacking to go to the beach with her.

" Okay, Erica. You can go if you promise me that you will stay right there," Marina told her. She pointed down from the living room to the sand below. " I don't want you to go past that wall."

She was pointing to the retaining wall some twenty feet from the front of the house.

" I won't ! I promise," Erica assured her mother.

Marina looked up at the loft bedroom and then looked farther up at the loft library, and realized that she could see Erica from almost any point at the front of the house. As long as she stayed on the strip of sand between the house and wall, she would be fine.

" Okay. I'll watch you from up there in the bedroom, have fun."

Erica ran to the kitchen to get the popcorn from Kathleen.

" Wait, wait, Erica," Marina called. " I need to put some lotion on you."

Erica was very fair skinned. A few minutes in the sun out on the white sand and Marina knew that Erica would burn up. Even in Kansas in the summertime, Erica would burn from the sun. Chris on the other hand was less sensitive to the sun. Much like Marina, who could lay in the sun all afternoon and not seem to burn at all. She had been known to lay by the pool for hours and never burn. David was always jealous of that fact. He, like Erica, would burn up in just a half an hour. Erica stopped in the hall and waited for Marina to go with her to the kitchen. There she took the suntan lotion and applied some to her face, arms and legs.

Marina hesitated for a second at the door and questioned her inner self as to whether she should let Erica out onto the beach, alone. She knew that Erica was very responsible and that she wouldn't go any closer to the beach than agreed. She also knew that Erica always listened.

" Be careful and stay close," Marina pleaded.

" I will Mom."

Erica wanted to wait until just the right moment to feed the gulls. She held her bag of popcorn close to her body and grasped the top of the plastic bag tightly. Marina watched from the huge windows as Erica came around to the front of the building. An occasional gull flew by and over Erica, continuing their flight along the beach, occasionally being lifted high in the sky by the updraft over the water. Erica watched the gulls for quite some time before she threw the first handful of corn to the wind. The ocean breezes took the corn from in front of her, and blew it over her head and onto the sand, far behind her. Erica brushed her long blonde hair from her face with her free hand and again grabbed another handful of popcorn. Turning to see if Marina was watching, she threw another handful of popcorn to the winds. This time the gulls came gliding across the beach and swooped closer to her. As if given a signal, they came from all over the beach. The first to arrive in front of Erica went directly to the sand. Quickly snatching the popcorn from the surface of the beach, then flying in a circle around her.

Erica had seen nothing like this before. First, there were a few gulls, then within seconds, there were fifty gulls. Within a minute, there were more than a hundred. There wings outstretched and their tail feathers lowered as they hovered around her. She could see their faces and their legs hanging down. Erica watched them against the bright blue sky until there were so many that she was under an umbrella of feathers in motion.

Inside the house, Marina watched as the gulls gathered around Erica. She was astonished as the number of gulls increased, until there was a cloud of gulls. They kept coming. There were so many that they created a wave as the wind blew across the sand under the hundreds of wings. Occasionally, a gull would leave the group and dart across the beach, only to quickly return to the group and fight its way to the front and to the popcorn being thrown to the air. Marina knew that Erica would be excited by just the sheer number of birds. It was all quite beautiful. Their black wing tips darting up and down made a fantastic display. Marina could hear her screaming in excitement from under the blanket of sea birds.

Marina turned to go up to the master bedroom to finish unpacking. From the corner of her eye, she saw a gull leave the group. Its wing feathers were red from what appeared to be fresh blood. At first she thought that maybe the birds had actually attacked each other in the feeding frenzy that was taking place. Soon, two other gulls raised from the group, and both were stained with the unmistakable bright red blood. A sense of panic gripped Marina. The screams from under the canopy of hovering birds grew louder as Erica shrieked in pain. The gulls were, in fact, attacking her.

" My God," Marina screamed as she started toward the door in a panic.

As she ran across the room, the high-pitched, unmistakable scream of a child grew louder and louder. That didn't stop the gulls. At first, they attacked individually, then in groups, ripping and tearing at Erica's flesh. Under the canopy of birds, she tried desperately to protect herself. In a panic she tried to run from the attackers. After dropping the remaining popcorn to the sand, she held her hands to her face, yet they continued to strike at her fingers and arms with their strong beaks. One gull would pull at her skin while the next would join in and begin to tear her young flesh. They began pulling the skin from her fingers like pulling the leaves from ears of corn. They continued the unrelenting strikes upon her soft skin, first puncturing her and then tearing. Like ripping clams from the shell, they tore with incredible force, not letting go until they had their portion of flesh. Each gull tried to tear its own piece of her skin. As one would manage to rip loose a piece of flesh, Erica would reach for the pained area with one hand. As soon as her exposed skin was revealed, the gulls struck her again and again at the freshly exposed area. As the puncture wounds on her body quickly filled with blood, they became more aggressive in their attack.

Marina rushed to the door, and after some trouble with the deadbolt latch, flung it open against the foyer wall. Outside, she heard more clearly the horrible sound of her daughter in agony, the screams that a mother instinctively knows. She couldn't get to Erica fast enough.

Erica's body couldn't take it any longer and she began to stumble. Not knowing what direction the house was made it all the more difficult for her. Turning and spinning under the cloud of attacking birds confused her. Her screams for help to her mother were muffled from under the hundreds and hundreds of gulls. Finally, she fell to the sand. Her small face, streaked with blood, splashed into the soft sand. The gulls continued their relentless attack. As Erica slipped into unconsciousness, the pain subsided. It made the attack all the more easier.

When Marina got to the cloud of birds, she covered her face and, while screaming Erica's name, fought her way to the limp body lying in the sand. At first, she couldn't find the ninety-pound body that was lying motionless.

From the inside of the house, Kathleen and Chris appeared at the window. Startled by the sound of Marina screaming, Kathleen rushed to the glass. At first, she couldn't see what was happening. The gulls continued swirling and diving into the cluster of other potential killers. There were thousands by this time. Erica had fallen beneath them and was lying still, critically wounded in the sand. Soon, Kathleen realized that there was blood on the birds and she could see Marina run under the awning of killers.

As Marina ducked and pushed her way through the beating feathers and wings, she looked feverishly for Erica. There, just a few more feet in front of her, was her beloved little girl. Gulls were still pulling and ripping on her skin, fighting each other for a piece a flesh like buzzards working on a dead carcass. They continued battling each other for the chance to get to the torso. Marina threw herself on the still body, covering Erica. She could see brief flashes of sunlight through the hovering birds as they continued to circle. Afraid to lift her head from the sand, she remained on top of Erica and gathered her arms under her body, like a football player covering a fumbled ball. The gulls continued shrieking and screaming overhead. Marina couldn't hold back the tears. Her tears blotted in the cool sand and caused it to stick to her face. Thinking of Erica lying under her and not making a sound frightened Marina more than anything had ever done before. Instinctively, she cried out, " Oh, God, ... please, no. Please, no."

Kathleen ran to the phone and dialed for help, while Chris ran to the open door. While waiting for an answer, she yelled out for Chris to stay with her.

" This is emergency, can I help you," the voice answered.

" Something terrible has happened. We need help," she pleaded.

" Can you give me your address?" the dispatcher asked.

The emergency number put Kathleen in touch with the dispatcher on the island. As soon as she answered the call, she pressed the button that would alert the fire company in the building next to the island's city hall where the dispatcher was located.

GULLS

" Ma'am, we need your address?" the voice asked again.

Kathleen managed to give the address to the dispatcher even though she was scared and not thinking clearly.

" That would be the Rutledge Place ... is that right ma'am?"the voice inquired.

Because the dispatcher was a resident of the island, and had lived there all of her life, she knew most all of the addresses that were given to her on the calls. But, Rutledge Place, was known to every resident of the island. At least known to any resident who had walked the south end of the island's beaches. When the house was being built, it was the conversation of both the year round residents, and the summer tourists as well. "... you say that the girl has been bitten by gulls? Is that correct ma'am?"

" Yes, that's right. Bitten all over by sea gulls," Kathleen told her.

Marina waited until the sound of the gulls had stopped. She could feel the warmth of the sun on her back and shoulders. She lifted her head slowly, just a few feet from her, she could see the gulls standing in the sand - waiting. All of them were facing her as if waiting for her to move. The wind pushed their feathers up on the back of their necks, making them look even more threatening. She couldn't stop sobbing. Her tears blurred her vision, but she could do nothing to hold back her tears or to brush away the sand. Marina knew that she would have to get Erica into the house. Somehow, she would have to make a run for it.

The gulls weren't making a sound. They stood watching - waiting, and every once in a while, they moved closer to Erica and Marina.

Marina carefully slid her left arm under Erica and tightly around her waist. Then, she placed her right arm across Erica's chest, digging it through the soft sand, and pushed her hand under Erica's armpit. If she ran with her pulled tightly to her body, she could probably make it before being overcome by the birds, she thought. Marina knew that it was a chance that she would have to take. She could feel the wetness of blood on both of Erica's arms and hands. She could also feel the grit of sand in Erica's open wounds. This was no time for a mistake. This was no time to stumble. Marina was afraid that if she gave the gulls another chance, they would devour both of them.

In one sweeping motion, Marina stood with Erica held tightly in her arms, and turned toward the house. As she started running,Erica began sliding from her grip, like a paper grocery bag falling from her arms. Marina couldn't control it. Please don't let this happen, she said to herself. The gulls lunged forward from the sand and were coming toward her at breakneck speed, taking to the air. Within seconds, their screaming started all over again. They took to the air once more and were determined to strike again at both of them. Marina felt the first gull hit her back.

She was stunned by the force of it but never faltered in her run.

Marina's first rushing steps through the sand, seemed to be slow. She couldn't get the right traction in the soft sand, and the gulls were getting closer and closer.

" Mom, run !" Christopher called from the doorway. "Run !" he screamed.

Marina squeezed Erica tightly against her body. If she dropped her, she felt that she wouldn't have a chance to pick her up again, before the gulls would overtake her. To Marina, it seemed that the house was too far away from her to outrun the gulls. In her mind, it was all happening in slow motion. One or two of the gulls, managed to get close enough that they struck Marina's body with their beaks. Marina couldn't tell the extent of the strike. She couldn't stop her running, but she felt the pain. A gull locked on to her blouse and dangled from her.

*

" Brigantine ONE, we have a pediatric, female, victim of a gull attack." the dispatcher said.

The firehouse doors opened, and the yellow fire truck began moving forward, manned by five people, two of which were paramedics. As the driver listened carefully for the address, his mental picture of the streets stopped when he heard the dispatcher say the Rutledge Place.

The one thing that he couldn't get a mental picture of was the report to him that the pediatric was a victim of a gull attack. His assessment of the call was that it's probably nothing more than a superficial wound and that a band-aid or two should handle it. He felt that this was hardly a call for emergency.

Marina ran as hard and as fast as she could. The gulls continued to dart and dive against her body, striking her with almost overwhelming force. She could feel the weight of them as they struck her body and she was surprised each time that they could hit with such force. At one point, she felt as though she was going to be pushed down in the sand. To balance her running, she knew that she would have to run faster. There was no motion from Erica. Marina couldn't tell if she was alive or dead. The house bobbed up and down in her vision as though the entire incident was taking place on film and the camera was bouncing. When Marina got to the door of the house, she felt she couldn't run another step and fell into the foyer. Much to her surprise, the gulls didn't try to enter. Christopher closed the tall door, shutting out the threat of further attack.

Marina lifted her body from on top of Erica, and quickly turned her over. There was no telling how many bites, punctures and tears she had experienced. It was easy to see that she was losing blood rapidly. Marina only had one place on her arm where a gull tried to grab. It still hurt more than Marina would have ever imagined. Just then, Marina could hear the sound of a siren.

" They're on their way," Kathleen told her. "That must be them I hear now."

Erica lay still on the polished marble floor. Her skin

was covered with blood and sand. Marina noticed that her lips were turning a bluish color. Quickly, she placed her ear to Erica's face. She could hear her faint breathing.

The fire and rescue team saw that the door to the house was partially open, so they called to Marina. She didn't want to leave the body of her daughter, lying helplessly on the floor, but there was little choice. So, when the team entered the foyer, she stood and backed away from the scene that she would never forget. Imprinted in her mind would always be the picture of her eleven-year-old girl, covered with blood and terrible wounds, motionless and limp with deep red blood dripping from her arms and neck.

Quickly, the para-medics evaluated the situation. Before they could attempt to stop the bleeding, they checked for her breathing and circulation. It was apparent that Erica was unconscious. Just how far into unconsciousness had to be determined. Andrew Baxter, twenty-four-year-old paramedic crouched over Erica's body. After turning her on her side to make certain that she would not choke from the blood that had trickled into her throat, he lifted her arm. Erica had no response to the pulling and move-ment of her body. The sound of her wet skin slapping onto the cold floor was a sound that Marina would never forget. Andrew Baxter's assistant, Denise, who was positioned at Erica's head, carefully pulled the long blonde hair from Erica's cheek. In a gentle motion, she stroked the little girls jaw bone and held her head gently in her hands. Denise was a mother of a ten-year-old girl. Pediatric emergency calls were always traumatic, but this one was almost more than she could bear. Andrew removed a pen from his shirt pocket. Placing it so the clip was directly on top of Erica's middle finger nail, he pressed the pen against her fingernail. Andrew knew that this was one of the more sensitive areas of the human body. After a little pressure was applied to her fingernail, Erica yanked her arm from him. It happened so quickly that it appeared to be a reflex action. Instead, it was an acknowledgement of the pain. Andrew and Denise looked at each other in agreement that Erica was only in a mild degree of unconsciousness. But there was no time to waste.

William Pell was still holding the twin engine jet helicopter on the landing pad at Atlantic City's General Hospital when the call came in. William was a vintage helicopter pilot from the VietNam war days. After retirement from the Marines, he took a position as flight instructor with Sikorski Aircraft Company and then dedicated his time as pilot for medical evac-uation team at Atlantic City. The voice in his headset called to him.

" Med Evac ONE, this is Brigantine Dispatch."

He watched the red flashing light on the instrument panel begin to blink. The emergency locator system would automatically direct him to the paramedics. The paramedics remained in the house with Erica. After pulling an antenna from the portable radio they had with them, they pressed the button that activated the signal. That signal was instantly picked up by the helicopter, and a digital number was displayed under the flashing light, the direction that Pell would fly the helicopter to get to Erica.

The two paramedic assistants entered the helicopter while Pell held the aircraft on the ground. As soon as the door was shut, he lifted the craft and turned it toward the signal. He was now flying a straight line that would take him directly to the south end of Brigantine Island and the awaiting paramedic team on the ground at the Rutledge Place.

As he cleared the strip of casino hotels of Atlantic City and swung the helicopter over the beach, he noticed the gulls that avoided the helicopter by diving toward the open sea below. In Pell's' mind, this was just another call, another "scene hit" as they were known. In the back of the helicopter, the paramedic team was getting the information that they needed from the ground. Erica had already been started on two IV's and they had positioned her on the stretcher. She was wrapped in a white blanket, but still, she was unconscious. Pell had been listening to the report that was being made from the ground. Attacked by gulls? He thought he may have been hearing things at first, but then it was confirmed again. The youth was attacked by gulls and considered critical.

Marina wanted to go with Erica and was assured by Denise that she would be going with the helicopter. Kathleen assured her that everything would be fine at the house until she got back, and " not to worry."

" Don't let Chris outside !" Marina yelled at Kathleen as she ran to the helicopter.

The sound of the helicopter blades cutting through the ocean wind could be heard long before it arrived over the beach. Slowly, it moved closer to the glass-walled house. Inside the house, they could hear the sand splashing against the glass as the helicopter got closer. The sound of the approaching jet engines and rotor noise caused the sea gulls who were responsible for the tragedy to quickly disperse. Like stalkers of prey, they had waited in the sand, watching from their vantage point on the beach, waiting patiently for another chance to strike at Erica. However, the helicopter was too much for them and, like gang members in the inner city, they fled the scene.

As the helicopter, with Erica and Marina inside, lifted from the beach. Kathleen and Chris stood inside the house watching. Chris had been crying terribly for Erica. What about Mr. Spencer, Kathleen asked herself. As the helicopter disappeared over the city, three miles away, Kathleen remained standing, still in shock over what she had just seen. Outside the house, the gulls had gathered again. One by one, they arrived. Landing on the beach, and facing the ocean breeze, each one occasionally crying out. That romantic sound that was so familiar to anyone who had been to the beach now became a warning call to Kathleen and Chris. The sound of gulls caused them to fear another possible attack. It gave them a cold chill.

CHAPTER THREE:
All-Over Tan

Only when the wind was coming from the ocean could Leslie Neill hear the sound of the breakers crashing onto the sand. On this morning, the sun was strong and the early morning breezes began to move the sea's cool air inland.

Leslie carefully slid from under the cotton sheets, so as to not awaken Jeff. They arrived on the island late the night before. After some love-making, they both fell fast asleep. If there was nothing else to their relationship, there was intense sex. They just hit it off, and could be as open an uninhibited as the modern day magazines would prescribe. Leslie couldn't imagine that part of the relationship getting any better. She was twenty-two, tall, with dark brown, almost black, hair. Her emerald green eyes captured everyone's attention. She was slender and well proportioned. Leslie rarely went unnoticed by the opposite sex.

Brigantine, was far from her home in Michigan. She

looked forward to the vacation and spending this time with Jeff. He had asked her repeatedly to marry him, but Leslie planned this trip to be the decision maker. They had their ups and downs in the relationship, and this would be the test. Jeff promised Leslie that he would curb his drinking and pay more attention to her. When he had asked her to marry him, she told Jeff that she needed some time to give him an answer. He didn't ask again after that time, almost six months ago. Leslie was sure that this would be the right time to answer him. If all went well, she would say yes.

She grabbed her short silk robe from the chair and put it on as she walked down the hall to the kitchen. Thinking about the intensity of their relationship caused her to day-dream as she filled the glass container for the coffee maker with water. There was no question in her mind about how much Jeff loved her. He always took the time to make her feel extra special, but marriage wasn't to be taken lightly. Almost every one of her friends had already been married and divorced within three years.

" It'll be just great sleeping with Miss America," Jeff said.

Leslie flinched when he put his arms around her and scared her half to death. She didn't hear him coming down the hall to the kitchen, nor did she hear him walk up behind her. So when he spoke, she reacted by gasping and flinching in his arms. He gently kissed the back of her neck. As she turned to face him, the robe opened, revealing her young and full body.

" Just remember which one of us is the Miss America, and that's if Tonya makes it," she replied.

Leslie was Tonya's identical twin sister. Tonya would be arriving in Atlantic City for the pageant in a few days. She would be staying until the pageant was over. Leslie talked Jeff into taking this extended vacation, and that way they could go to the pageant in hopes of watching her sister win and become Miss America. No one could tell them apart from each other. Leslie and Tonya always had fun switching roles and fooling people. They had the same voices, the same smile, and the same mannerisms - they had the same everything, except for one small detail. When they were young and someone would comment about how identical they were, their mother would always respond that there was only one sure way of telling them apart. But the unique way was always kept a secret. Leslie had two deep dimples on the cheeks of her buttocks that Tonya didn't have. Neither had any distinguishable marks anyplace else. If they wore the right bathing suits it was obvious. But, their favorite bathing suits were one piece, which covered the tell tale dimples of which Leslie was so proud.

" I'm sure Tonya will win," Jeff continued. " After all, she is by far the best-looking of them all. And both of you are so damned smart and talented, I can't see where anyone else could compare."

" Just don't be making love to me and fantasizing on making it with Miss America,"

Being Miss Michigan was very important to Tonya and she had her hopes of winning the pageant in

GULLS

Atlantic City. Both Tonya and her sister handled disappointments very well. Leslie was sure that if Tonya didn't win, she would make the best of it and move on to her career in communications.

Jeff had Leslie pulled hard against his body. With his right hand, he pushed the small of her back until her body formed and molded to his.

" Not now," she said.

She had planned on spending the day at the secluded end of the island. In order to do so, she would have to get a lot done. Jeff planned on spending the day on the golf course. Leslie couldn't believe that someone could go to the beach and spend the first day on the golf course, fifteen miles from the ocean. Her plans, however, were to take the three-mile walk to the secluded end of the island and begin to get her "all over tan".

" Okay," Jeff replied. " Besides we don't have time, not if I want to get on the course early."

" You can get dressed. I'll get us something for breakfast and you'll be out of here in half an hour."

After breakfast, Jeff didn't waste any time getting in their car and heading for the country club in Atlantic City. As soon as he left Leslie put on her bathing suit and then pulled on a pair of red nylon running shorts. She had already packed her small cooler with a sandwich, some fruit, and three diet Cokes.

After covering them with some ice from the refrigerator she closed the lid. In her beach bag she was careful to put three of her favorite magazines and a paperback novel, "Hunted". She also checked the boom box to make sure that the batteries were strong enough. Her plans were to spend the entire day at the beach and she didn't want to have the batteries run low. She took four additional batteries from her suitcase and put them in the beach bag.

Leslie had been to Brigantine Island many times before. Her parents used to rent a house on the island for vacations every year. So she considered this almost routine. This year, her parents were staying in Atlantic City at one of the big hotels. That way they could be right where the action was during the week of the pageant.

She was careful to make sure that the key to the beach house was tightly fastened to her beach bag strap, and after pulling the door to the house shut, she turned toward the breeze and headed for the beach.

The sun was getting much stronger as Leslie walked the beach. To her left, she was bordered by the soft sand dunes. To her right, the ocean continuously slid toward her and then quickly retreated, soon to be replenished again by the salt water as the tide edged its way farther up the beach. Leslie saw the tops of bayberry bushes on the other side of the dunes and she knew there were many secluded places in which she could spend the afternoon, sunning in the nude. As she walked toward them, the sound of the ocean became softer and more distant behind her. The bushes on the other side were thick and she had to walk along the top ridge of the sand dunes until she could find an opening in the branches that would give her sufficient room to enter. Once doing so, she found herself in an area surrounded by the thick bushes. This most secluded of places would allow her to spend the day in quiet and comfortable sun bathing.

Having selected the right spot, she carefully placed her radio and cooler in the sand and spread her blanket on the hard but still cool sand. Because of the protection from the ocean breezes, the sand under these bushes was level and smooth. The openings in the branches allowed an area of ten feet or more to be clear. This would stay sunny for the day. Leslie was sure that she would probably get too much sun by the time she left the beach in the late afternoon. She gave one last look around to be certain that the space she had chosen would be secluded enough.

Feeling sure and comfortable with the spot, she placed her thumbs into the elastic waistband of her nylon running shorts and the bottom of her bikini and pulled them down to her ankles. Carefully, she placed both of them on top of the radio. Reaching behind her, she unsnapped the top to her bathing suit and threw it on top of the cooler. With her toe on the right foot, she pushed her running shoe off her left foot, then quickly followed with the other. Before lying on the blanket, she took her sunscreen lotion and began at her shoulders and spread it evenly on both arms.

After squeezing some into the palm of her hand, she gently spread it over her breasts and on her stomach. While the sounds of the ocean continued in the background and the summer sun shone directly overhead, Leslie finished preparing for the relaxing afternoon and carefully lay on the white soft blanket.

She could feel the warmth of the sun on her neck and on her pale untanned buttocks. As she opened her paperback novel, she thought of how wonderful it felt and how peaceful this was. She stretched her body over to the radio, and tuned into the first radio station that had music. The oldies radio station format was perfect. She was careful not to turn it too loud, so that no one would hear the music from the other side of the sand dunes.

Because the secluded and protected place was away from the breeze and the beach, it soon became hot and her body began to heat.Rapidly her skin became tepid and beads of moisture collected on the surface. It felt good to her. And the combination of the lotion on her body with the odor from the salt air drifting across her from the ocean brought back the pleasant memory from the last time she had been here.

While lying quietly in the sun and reading her book, Leslie didn't pay much attention to the gulls that had gathered overhead. Soon, she recognized their familiar sounds, but she paid little notice. Their wings cast flickering shadows across the pages of the book and shortly it became a distraction to her reading. She glanced upward. There were hundreds of them. At first, her thoughts were that they were just curious and that they would soon move away. As she half turned upward to get a better look, the sun blinded her. As soon as she began to shield her eyes from it with her right hand, the gulls began the attack. As though she had given them a signal, they dived at her naked body. The shock of the first bite caused her to give a loud scream.

She had walked almost a mile from the nearest populated beach, so her screams were not heard. From her spot in the dunes, her additional cries for help were deadened by the sand and the sound of the oceans waves pounding the beach.

Leslie had no time to try to reach her running shorts. The best that she could do was to try and pull the blanket around her and protect herself from their attack. The gulls seemed to have sensed that she was trying to cover herself and quickly they began striking her face and head. As one would dive and strike her, attempting to tear some flesh, the next would wait angrily for the chance. Quickly, she covered her face with her hands and, just as quickly, they struck her breasts, her side, her legs, and her back. Soon she was covered with them. Like buzzards gathering around a fallen and wounded animal, they piled on top of her, each fighting for a space on her body. It didn't take long before they had broken her skin, and blood began covering large areas of her moistened skin.

She thought about the bayberry bushes and how she would have to try and take cover under the branches. Blinded by the combination of tears and blood that filled her eyes, she began desperately crawling and feeling her way for cover. The jagged branches of the wild bushes added to the pain as they caught on the already torn flesh. Leslie knew that she would have to try and continue but she was still coherent enough to know that she couldn't possibly go the distance. She couldn't out maneuver the gulls. Thinking that getting under the branches would stop the air attack she quickly scrambled for the bushes. But the killers continued along the ground, darting at her, and each time managing to pull pieces of flesh from her torn body. The pain was excruciating. At times she felt ice cold and then it burned as though there was a torch being held to her. As more of the nerves became exposed, the more it felt cold. A gathering of gulls at her feet were repeatedly attacking the soft underside of her foot as it became exposed with each helpless attempt of crawling from them.

Their shrieking and screaming continued under the bushes as they followed her like a posse of killers. Leslie somehow continued on. For almost a hundred yards, she crawled through the sand and bushes. They had bitten almost every inch of her exposed body before she finally fell, face down, in the soft sand. One gull had grabbed a vain from under the ripped skin. With the help of another, they pulled on it. It snapped back many times like uncooked chicken. Eventually they managed to tear it from her arm and then fight over the morsel.

As her last shallow breath departed her lungs, a cloud covered the hot sun above her, above the sand dunes, above the island, and above the gulls. As though given another signal, a signal that they had finished a task, they scurried in all directions across the sand from under the bushes and wherever there was an opening.

GULLS

Leslie was left lying in the sand as the blood trickled from her and blotted through the sand granules, soon drying and hardening in the summer heat. The gulls were quickly attracted to another part of the island. A little more than a mile to the south, the beaches were lined with families, bathing in the sun and with children splashing in the surf. No one would know of the attack the gulls had just made. They returned to circle and dive over the sunny beaches, sailing over the children at play and swooping out over the breakers.

*

At the south end of the island, Byron Jackson crouched over the nest of a puffin family. After replacing the grass and twigs that hid the three small eggs from the view of predators, Byron stood and made some notations in the notebook he always carried with him. Six feet eight inches tall, and weighing just over three hundred pounds, Byron certainly couldn't be considered a light-weight, by any stretch of the imagination. The recent graduate of Miami University was now working on his Master's degree. The summer job on Brigantine Island with the National Wildlife Federation would complete his research on sea birds, and help for his completing his Masters. His mother was a native of Saigon, VietNam, and his father was born in New Jersey. They had met during the war, fell deeply in love, and Byron was conceived during their courtship. However, his father was killed in the war, and after a struggle of five years,Byron was eventually sent to live in New Jersey with his grandmother - One of the many AmerAsians from the war, but one lucky enough to be sent to America. He excelled in every-thing he did. Winning a football scholarship from a northern New Jersey high school enabled him to attend the University of Miami. Many remembered Byron from the Orange Bowl game that helped place Miami as the number one team in the nation.

Byron had a deep love for birds and wildlife. He had been ridiculed throughout his early childhood for being a bird watcher, a stereotype that carried with it constant remarks about his masculinity, but he con-tinued studying the thing he loved the most. He never feared for his masculinity or his sexual identity as a result of being classified as a " bird watcher".

Returning to his Jeep, which was parked in the sand dunes on the southern end of the island, Byron fin-ished making the necessary notations concerning the birds that were soon to hatch a family of three.

He had been carefully observing the family of puffins for almost two weeks and they would be hatching the eggs soon. Puffins, were not known to be seen in this part of the world and having eggs to hatch at this time of the year was highly unusual. It was rare to see them that far south. Before finishing his round of the preserve, he would be checking on the nests of the Black Skimmer, the Least Tern and the Piping Plover. All of these were on the endangered species list and it was Byron's job to monitor them.

As he started the engine of his Jeep, the cellular phone rang.

" This better be good," he said, immediately after placing the phone to his face.

" Byron, this is Rick. The strangest damned thing has just taken place on the island. Get this - a girl, a young girl, was attacked by gulls." he told Byron. "They say she was feeding them popcorn on the beach, when they, for no damned reason, attacked her."

Rick was back at the headquarters on the south end of the island. He and Byron had today's duty, and would take shifts, driving the entire length of the Brigantine island, making sure that the National Wildlife Preserve at the north was secure. Byron was now headed along the beach in his direction. " Are you sure she was attacked by the gulls?" Byron quizzed.

" That's what I'm told. Look, I'm heading over to the residence now. I'll meet you there,"

" Where's, there ...?" Byron asked.

" The Rutledge Place," Rick answered.

Byron had only been on the island for a little more than six weeks, but he already knew exactly where the Rutledge Place was. While returning the phone to its cradle, He pressed down on the gas pedal, and the Jeep responded immediately. As the Jeep continued along the harder wet sand along the water's edge, he passed a young couple, swimming naked in the breakers. The girl never noticed the Jeep speeding along the sand. With her back to Byron, she dove into the ocean. Normally, he would stop and advise the two bathers that they could not swim in the ocean at this part of the island, and that they would have to swim on the south side of the pier where there were lifeguards. This had always been a problem at the island. People felt that if the north end of the island was, in fact, a government reservation, that they, as taxpayers, should automatically be permitted to swim from those beaches. The south end of the island, that was divided by a pier required beach tags. Those beach tags had to be purchased by everyone using the beach. Often people from the city would drive out to the island, park their car on a side street, and walk through the sand dunes to the wildlife preserve and use the beaches there.

Byron went speeding past the two swimmers. He would arrive at the Rutledge Place at about the same time as Rick. In his mind, he tried to recall if he had ever heard of a sea gull attack on a human. As strange as it seemed, Byron felt something wrong in the pit of his stomach - something odd, something urgent, something eerie.

✳

At the Atlantic City Convention Center, David walked with his office manager, Suzette Feazell. They had a lot of ground to cover, while checking out the competition. Every major manufacturer of computer hardware and software, was represented at the show. They knew that it would take at least three days to see it all.

Although Suzette didn't have much responsibility for the marketing of computers, the show would give her the opportunity to meet some of the people that she had spoken with on the phone. David also took the opportunity to spend some time with her. She was a very attractive girl of twenty-three years old. Suzette knew that she was pretty and made sure that she wore the proper clothing that would accentuate her shapely body. David was more than proud to walk with her and introduce her to people that she would have most likely spoken with when calling the company. David's relationship with Marina was so strong. Suzette was absolutely no threat to Marina. But David wouldn't ever pass up the chance to spend time with her. They were a good working team and also good friends outside the office.

While walking from one display booth to the other, they were approached by a runner. The young boy in his early teens carried a pink slip in his right hand and a note pad fastened on the top of a wooden yard stick, in his left hand. David Spencer was written in bold, black letters. This was the method that the convention center used to locate people at the show. The runners worked for tips and they were known to make as much as three hundred dollars a day if they were aggressive and fast enough. The boy held the handmade sign, high above his head, and came down the carpeted isle toward David.

" David, there's a message for you," Suzette told him.

" I'm David Spencer," he told the runner.

Without saying anything, the boy handed David the pink slip. Written on the note was the message.

" Emergency, call Marina at the Atlantic City Hospital, 555-8897."

"Suzette, help me find a phone. It's an emergency!" David didn't even have time to give the boy a tip. Instead, he left the runner and Suzette and headed toward the outside wall of the convention center. He couldn't imagine what could be wrong. He looked down at the note that he got from the runner, but there was no time recorded. David thought that it could have taken hours for them to locate him. Looking quickly over his shoulder for Suzette, all he could see was a sea of people behind him. Suzette was sure to catch up with him at some point, but he didn't have time to worry about that now.

It took David some time to find the phones that were located in the main lobby of the center. Marina remained calm as she told David what had happened. Immediately, he grabbed a taxi cab from outside the convention center and slamming the rear door of the cab, David yelled, " Atlantic City Hospital, and hurry."

*

When Byron arrived at the Rutledge Place, he saw

that Rick was already there. The other department Jeep was parked against the sand dune to the left of the main door of the house. A flock of sea gulls took to the air as Byron pulled onto the soft sand and closer to the house. Seeing the gulls take to the wind and struggle to stabilize their flight caused Byron to question again the possibility of gulls attacking.

Inside, Kathleen calmly told Rick and Byron of what had happened. Chris would add comments about just how bad Erica had been torn up by the attacking gulls.

" I gave a full report to the police, just a moment ago, ya know," Kathleen told them. " I can tell you this, I won't be goin' out to the beach again, nor will the boy, I can assure ya."

" Well, ma'am, I'm sure this is just a freak incident. Sea gulls aren't known to attack humans. I doubt if it will ever happen again," Byron told her. " Do me a favor though - have Mr. or Mrs. Spencer call me at this number. I would like to talk with them about the incident. Anything we can find out will be a help," Byron said.

After leaving Kathleen and Christopher, Byron and Rick stood for a long time by their Jeeps, talking about the incident.

" I can tell you this," Byron told him. "In some parts of the world, they call gulls rats with wings, but I never heard of them attacking people. Aggressive, maybe. Stalkers, that's for damned sure, but not what you would call attackers. Maybe we better get ready for all hell to break loose if gulls start to attack people," he continued.

" Yea, well, if this girl is as torn up as that woman tells us, maybe we had better be ready for all hell to break loose," Rick responded.

" I'm going back to headquarters," Byron told him. " I'll go through my text-books and maybe find out something. I could have missed something in the behavior of sea gulls, but I don't think so."

As Rick stood with his one foot on the side rail of his Jeep, he had one more question for Byron. " Look, Byron, you are the expert on sea birds, especially gulls. Could these things get even more aggressive, once they have had the taste of human flesh? You know, like the shark or say... the lion?" he asked.

" I doubt it," Byron answered. " But, before we start jumping to conclusions, let's make sure that this was an aggressive attack and not something provoked by the girl."

✳

When David arrived at the hospital and to Erica's room, he was met by Marina and Dr.White. Marina spotted David as soon as the elevator door opened and immediately ran to him.

" It was terrible," she cried out. " They tried to kill her, they were killing her! Hundreds of them, all over her."

" How is she?" David asked.

" She's still unconscious, and the doctor said she has

lost an awful lot of blood," Marina continued. " But he thinks she'll be okay. We just have to wait and see."

David continued to the door of Erica's room. Scared of what he would see yet knowing that he must be strong, he went into the room with Marina at his side. Erica lay there, motionless. The monitor screen displayed her heart-beat in an erratic series of lines. The sound that matched the picture of Erica's heart-beat was weak. This was the first time that Erica had been injured and the first time that she was in a hospital. Marina and David had been very lucky that since the children were born. They had never been injured to the point that they would have to even so much as see a doctor. But this scene was so very familiar, one that had been seen on TV many, many times. Plastic tubes filled with fluid led to Erica's arms. A white plastic clip had been placed on her second toe of her left foot. It was glowing with a red light. This was a method that was used to measure the amount of oxygen in her blood. Both of her hands were wrapped in gauze bandages.

" There has been considerable damage," the doctor said as he approached David. " Also, there is still a big chance for infection to set in. Gulls, you know, are scavengers, so we have to be careful with infection. She's on a very strong antibiotic."

Marina held on to David's arm with her face pressed against his shoulder. She could not stop crying. Through the tears and as difficult as it was, she continued to tell David of the horror.

The trip to the ocean that she had looked forward

to for so long was a grave mistake. Perhaps a mistake of a lifetime for Erica. David also thought that this was horrible, but how could sea gulls possibly do this? He grew up on the island. In all his life, he had never heard of any such thing.

*

At four o' clock that morning, Lyle Steele wasn't what you would call the greatest conversationalist. The light from his Volvo station wagon peered through the early morning fog as Lyle parked his car in front of his boat slip. Leaving his headlights on, he opened the back of the wagon and removed two styrofoam ice coolers and a small cardboard box of supplies for the trip. Waiting on the pier, was Robert Lance, Lyle's friend and fishing partner. It had always been their rule to leave on fishing trips no later than five in the morning, usually before the sun came up. The twenty-foot Cris Craft boat sat tied and waiting for them this morning.

Lyle was deep in thought about something he had heard on the morning news as he lifted the styrofoam coolers from the tail-gate of the car and carried them toward the boat.

" It's about fucking time," Robert said to him through the darkness.

" Jesus, Bob. You scared the shit out of me," Lyle said as he stumbled on the uneven boards of the pier.

GULLS

" Sorry, you old fart," Robert answered.

The two had been friends for over a decade. Each lived on the island and went fishing almost every chance they got. Both were retired and other than family obligations, they could go fishing almost every day. It became routine that each would bring the necessary items for the boat. Lyle's responsibility was for the food and other items. So, in the cardboard box he had a roll of toilet paper, some aspirin, a bottle of Bromo Seltzer, two rolls of paper towels, three spray cans of bug spray for the annoying mosquitoes in the bay and a plastic bottle of sun-tan lotion. Some of the items he bought at the local store while others he gathered from around the house. The two coolers were filled with beer and sandwiches that Lyle's wife, Nancy, had made the night before. She was sound asleep when Lyle had left. To her, his fishing trips were considered a godsend. She had given up many years before trying to get him to do anything to their small cottage on the island. So, instead of fighting with him, she just let him do what ever he wanted. After all, she thought, he did put in forty years in a factory in Philadelphia, making ball bearings. So, his retirement should mean that he could take it easy.

" The next time it's your turn to buy the supplies, fuck face, make sure that you get some decent beer, not that cheap, light shit you got the last time," Lyle instructed.

" Like it makes any difference. Like you wouldn't drink it anyway. It gets so fuckn' hot out there sometimes, I think I could drink sea water, and you would too," Robert responded.

To the east, the sky was just beginning to change color. Instead of the blackness of night blanketing the bay, the sky was beginning to turn turquoise. By the time they made sure they had everything they needed, the sky began to have the pink color of morning, indicating that it would be another hot summer day on the water.

" God damn it, Robert ! would you put that thing away and let's go," Lyle called out.

Robert decided to take a leak off the pier and Lyle could hear the unmistakable sound of water hitting on water from more than three feet above. " Besides, you ignorant shit, fish have to swim and make love in there," Lyle added.

"Yea, yea, I hear ya'. Just start that thing and let's get going," Robert answered.

Lyle turned the key to the engine with his right hand, pushing and pulling the throttle with his left hand, and after some argument by the starter, the gas engine finally came to life. Quickly, Lyle throttled back to the point that the engine was barely running. Robert zipped his pants and jumped down onto the boat. Somewhat rushing to the front, he untied the old Cris Craft and pushed the nose of the boat from the pier.

" Get ready, Lyle," he said jokingly. " I'm going to cut her loose. Hang on to her. Don't let this speed boat get away from you."

Robert was referring to the fact that the engine was so old that the boat may not make it through the inlet

GULLS

to the ocean. The two of them did repairs to the old boat themselves. Every once in a while, the engine would over-heat and they would have to sit out at sea for hours until they could finally get it started again. They did carry the necessary radios on board, but neither of them liked using them. As a last resort, they might consider radioing for help, but in all the years they fished together, they never did. Once they stayed out at sea all night and half into the next day. As long as there was food and beer on board,they wouldn't think of radioing for any assistance.

After untying the back of the boat, it gently moved across the calm bay water in the direction of the bridge that led from the island to Atlantic City. Until they were past the bridge, the water remained calm. At the entrance to the ocean, not far from the bridge, the water got rougher. Lyle waited until then to advance the throttle. In the meantime, they got there fishing equipment ready, and opened their first can of cold beer.

" Damn it, Lyle. You did it again."

" Did what, again," Lyle answered.

" Look. Over there. Aren't they your headlights?"

" God damn it ! How many times does this make?" Lyle asked as he watched a pair of lights in the distance get smaller and smaller.

" Shit head. I think it's a hundred or more."

Lyle had left the light of his Volvo on. When they returned it would be to a dead battery. Meanwhile, as they moved toward the bridge they both continued bickering and laughing about the car.

They usually went the same route. Out to the ocean in a straight line for a mile or so, then they would turn north and follow the coast line for forty or fifty miles, then they would return the same way. Except, on the way back they would fish off the coast of the island. Lyle would have the boat engine just running enough to keep them from entering the breakers and they would fish in the surf and watch the young girls walking the beaches of Brigantine Island. If the beer and sandwiches held out, they would fish until dark. With as much beer as they had on board, Lyle was sure they wouldn't return until late in the evening or later that night. While Erica lay in the hospital and Leslie lay on the beach, Lyle and his fishing partner drifted slowly on the ocean guzzling one beer after another to keep cool in the hot August sun.

✳

David and Marina remained at the hospital waiting for things to change for Erica. David was now finishing his tenth cup of coffee from the vending machine and was staring at the Atlantic City skyline off in the distance. The buildings were illuminated by the strong sunlight.

It had been a long day of waiting and worrying but he was relieved that Erica was conscious and awake. She would survive the ordeal. Marina was still in the room with her, talking to her and trying to comfort

Erica's mind. Occasionally, Erica screamed as she relived the horrible experience of the previous day. Even though she was heavily drugged, she had flash backs of the attack.

After a consultation with Dr. White, they decided to return to the island and to get some much-needed sleep. Both of them sat quietly in the back seat of the taxi cab as it turned into the driveway of the house, knowing that they would have to stay at Brigantine until Erica was out of the hospital. As far as Marina was concerned, they could just as well leave for Kansas today. They were told that Erica would be in the hospital for at least two weeks and then they would have to continue some therapy and treatment for an additional time. Christopher ran to his mother as soon as they opened the door.

David made himself a drink and returned again to the tall windows facing the ocean. He thought to himself that this was a grave mistake. He felt that they should have never come to the island. Never before, had he heard such a bizarre thing, getting attacked by gulls. There must have been a reason. David was just too tired to sort out the entire matter. Erica was the reflection of her mother. They had very much the same personality and the same sense of humor. She was very close to David and the term "pride and joy" was an under-statement.

David couldn't help himself. The combination of being tired and the trauma of the incident caused him to break into uncontrollable tears. He stood quietly, looking out at the ocean, and at the occasional

glimpse of a gull flying by. They didn't break his con-
centration on the memories of Erica, lying in the hospital, fighting for her life. He knew that he had better
soon get some sleep. Marina was consoling Chris in
the guest bedroom and telling him that Erica would
be home soon.

Marina and David slept close that night, neither
saying a word about the day's tragedy.

CHAPTER FOUR:
Media Frenzy

Third Street South on the island was lined with small summer beach cottages. In the middle of the first block, away from the beach, was the headquarters for the Brigantine Island Beach Patrol. Most of the lifeguards were students employed for the summer. All had graduated from the school of life preservation in Atlantic City and, by now, had been settled into the routine of the summer and the vacation resort. Early that morning, they had gathered, as usual, for their briefing. Taking his place in the front of the storage building, that also served as a meeting hall for the guards, was the guard chief. This was his fifteenth year as a life guard on the island and his third year as their leader.

" Listen up !" he yelled.

The room became instantly quiet. An Army drill sergeant couldn't ask for a better nor quicker response.

GULLS

" There's been an attack by gulls on the south end of the island," he stated. " A young girl. No one knows why, but she was severely attacked by the gulls and is now in critical condition in the hospital," he continued.

As the room became loud with the comments that the guards were making with each other, Commander Bill King jumped up on an upside down lifeboat that was against the wall in the front of the room.

" Listen up, damn it !" he continued.

" This could be very serious shit. Why they attacked the girl is still unknown, but they did. I want all of you to be on the lookout for anything suspicious. Anything that looks like it could be an attack. Keep your eyes open, leave the beach bunnies alone, and pay close attention. This could be something real freaky and it could never happen again, but ... listen up! If you see anything even remotely looking like an attack by those flying rats, call for help and get the victim out of there."

The Commander wasn't one for allowing horseplay or having his "people" as he referred to them spend their time talking with the hundreds of young girls that would walk the beach and stop at the lifeguard stands along the way. He was an expert on sneaking up on them in his four-wheel drive and giving an immediate reprimand to whomever the culprit might be. He was a good leader and prided himself with having the lowest accident rate on any of the New Jersey beaches.

" I'm sure this is some kind of rare occurrence, and that the kid might have even provoked them somehow," he continued. "But, just keep your eyes open. That's it ! Get out of here ! Hit the beaches !"

By ten o'clock in the morning, the beaches were filled. Two lifeguards maintained a watch from their elevated shacks that were positioned at every one hundred yards. The red flags that they would plant in the sand designated the width of the shore that they would allow swimmers. Young girls would walk in pairs along the shoreline, making certain that they could be seen by the equally young guards.

After positioning the lifeboat on rollers to keep it off the sand and to make it easy and quick to push into the water if necessary, the guards climbed to the loft seat in the shack and scanned the breakers. Occasionally, they would have to blow their whistles to give warning to swimmers that would drift out of the designated swimming areas. Now they had to also keep a watchful eye behind them, and search over the hot sands of the beaches for anything that might look suspicious.

The sun's hot rays on the almost snow white sand caused the heat to rise and distort the image of people on the beach. Tony Mouer and Mike Vance strained their eyes through their binoculars looking both north and south along the beaches. They could hardly make anything out in detail. The heat rising from the beach made the images look like mirage's. Only the things that were close to them were really clear. Each time they would hear loud children playing, they would lift the glasses to their face and strain to see.

GULLS

" Check it out !" Mike called.

Tony turned in the same direction to the south and he thought that there was no doubt about it.

" Holy shit !" he answered.

Immediately, the two jumped from the loft seat. Mike jumped on the "four wheeler" and started it with the key. Before the engine even had a chance to come alive he began pushing it forward with his feet to help get it rolling. Tony couldn't leave the stand. He would have to remain until help arrived.

Mike saw hundreds of gulls hovering over one spot on the beach. This was seen dozens of times during the day as children fed the gulls. Mike thought to himself that this looked like too many gulls and they were still coming. As he held the throttle of the four wheeler wide open and raced toward them, people heard him coming and parted from the beach in front of him. Occasionally, he would have to swerve to avoid hitting someone. To the right and left of him, the gulls were racing to the same location. The gulls did not waiver from their intentions. Instead, they slid in front of him, as if to be acknowledged that they had indeed won the race.

Under the canopy of wings and beaks were three children, each with a bag of popcorn. Mike slid the wheeler directly up to them, almost hitting some gulls on the way. The children stopped throwing the corn into the air, but the gulls continued the endless circling overhead. Within seconds, their parents came running up to the encounter.

" What's wrong?" asked the man as he grabbed the

arm of the young girl.

" Nothing, I guess," Mike answered.

" Nothing! What the hell's wrong with you? You come down the beach like a bat out of hell. Scared the wits out of everybody. Damn near hit us on the way, and all you can say is nothin', I guess?"

" I'm sorry. I thought there was something wrong. I... I heard the kids yelling. I thought someone might be hurt," Mike apologized.

" Bullshit ! You didn't hear any yelling from these kids. Not from all the way up there on the other beach."

" Forget it, Frank," the woman who had just walked up on them added.

" I'm sorry, Mister," Mike added. " I really did think something was wrong."

Coming toward them along the beach with the red lights flashing was the orange blazer driven by Commander King. Tony had used their radio to call for backup as instructed. Mike felt a little better that he would have some help from the commander. The blazer slowly drove closer to them and stopped.

" Oh, the hell with it," the man responded. "C'mon, kids. It's time to eat anyway."

With that remark, he took the three children and, along with the woman, they turned and headed toward their beach blanket and umbrella.

Mike got off the four-wheeler and approached Commander King.

" I really thought it was something. There were hun-dreds of gulls down here. More than I have ever seen at one time. I really thought ..."

" Don't worry about it, Mike," the Commander said. "I just hope we don't have to respond to every gathering of gulls on this beach or we won't have much time to do anything else. You did what you were supposed to do. You did the right thing. He'll cool off. Hell, an hour from now, he'll forget all about it. It will give him something to talk about tonight over pizza."

" Commander, are we to check it out every time we see these gulls swarming around something?" Mike asked.

" I'm afraid so, at least for right now. We don't have any way of knowing, so we had better if it looks like something."

" I've talked with the mayor and we're having some signs made - Do not feed the gulls. Mike, you're not the first. Hell, I've checked out nine of these within the last two hours. When we post the signs tomorrow, it should put an end to most of it. Of course, there will always be some smart ass that will feed them anyway," he said.

"Well, they will be easy to spot if they do," Mike added.

" Trouble is, we can't fine them for feeding the gulls. We're just going to try and bluff them with the signs. If we post them on all the beaches, and put the signs on all the shacks, trash cans, life boats, it might get the message across."

" I sure hope they find out what is causing the problem so we can get back to just watching the surfers," Mike said.

" I imagine we'll find out something soon," Commander King concluded.

✳

While at hospital Marina spent her entire time with Erica, taking only short breaks to get something to drink.

Erica was conscious, but sleeping a lot more than Marina would have thought. The doctors told her that her daughter was still in guarded condition, and that she had lost a lot of blood. There could be the problem with infection setting in from the gulls. Marina tried reading magazines while she was waiting with Erica, but she couldn't focus on much of anything.

Marina thought that watching the television might take her mind off of all that was happening, so she reached over to the hospital bed and pushed the button marked TV.

The network news was more than half finished. Marina sat in the chair next to the bed with Erica and stared out at the tall buildings of Atlantic City. In the background, she listened to the news anchor, Hal Edson.

" On the beaches in the south of France, bathers have been more than a little surprised by the unexpected and relentless attacks made by sea gulls," the announcer said. " More than six people enjoying the afternoon sun at the beach have been taken to nearby hospitals for severe bites caused by gulls. Although there seems to be no explanation for the attacks, authorities speculate that the problem may be caused by overfeeding of the gulls and their dependency on food from vacationers," he continued.

Marina didn't turn to the television when the report began. Not until the story finally worked its way into her consciousness and bring her to attention did she realize what she was hearing.

The screen filled with the unmistakable picture of the Mediterranean Sea. The images switched to the beaches and the shoreline. As usual, the camera focused on the couples walking the beach in their scant bathing suits. Then the camera focused on the dozens of sea gulls that lined the beaches.

" We now switch you to Mike Todd, standing by in France, with some more on this unusual and scary situation," the anchor said.

" Thank you, Hal," the reporter said. " This is perhaps the most unusual situation that has ever taken place on these beaches. I am told by authorities that it has never happened before. This afternoon's attack by the gulls on bathers had by all reports, been unprovoked. The victims came down here to the beach as they had done - some of them for as long as two weeks - and without warning, the gulls appeared and viciously attacked them. Authorities here speculate that the gulls had been over-fed by the vacationers. When the food supply was turned off, they became just a little more than aggressive, causing what seems to be serious injury to as many a six vacationers."

" Mike, have you heard of any other attacks that might have taken place on the beaches of Europe?" Hal asked.

" No, Hal, I haven't. I think that this may have been just a freak incident. Meanwhile, the bathers aren't turning their backs on these beautiful and common creatures. As you can see, the sunbathers are keeping a watchful eye on the feathered friends," he ended.

While Marina was entranced by the report, a nurse entered the room to take some blood samples from Erica. She stood by the bed facing the TV, amazed by what she had just heard.

" Can you believe this?" she said to Marina.

The television screen returned to the network news desk and to Hal Edson.

" We also have this report from our affiliate station WATL Atlantic City, New Jersey."

" It seems that a eleven-year-old girl on Brigantine Island, New Jersey, was attacked just yesterday by a flock of sea gulls. This attack was also unprovoked and the girl is hospitalized and in fair condition in Atlantic City. We will follow up on these reports and have them to you as soon as we can," the anchor concluded.

The television screen went to graphics of the network and to a commercial.

" Oh, my God," the nurse said in a whisper. " Every reporter in the country will be headed this way."

"What?" Marina asked.

" I hope the hospital is prepared to deal with this, because probably as we speak, they're headed for us," she added.

" I'm not going through a media feeding frenzy," Marina said. " I can't put my daughter through constant badgering by reporters. I just won't have it. Somebody had better tell them that I will not have Erica subjected to any kind of harassment by news hungry reporters looking for cheap headlines."

Just then the telephone by the bed rang. The nurse reached for it and answered.

" Yes, Ma'am, she's right here," the nurse answered. " It's for you Mrs. Spencer. She'd like to speak with you."

Marina went to the phone. " This is Marina," she answered.

" I'm sorry ta' be bother' you ma'am," Kathleen said. " But, the house is crawlin' with reporters. They started showin' up about a half hour ago. Insisted, they did, that I call you. I'll have nothin' ta say to them .. nothin' at all. Why, they have these huge cameras set up outside the house, ma'am," Kathleen told her.

" Don't you worry Kathleen. Keep them out of the house. I'll have David or somebody get over there and try to deal with them."Meanwhile, ask them to leave. If they don't, then call the police and have them thrown out."

While Marina was instructing Kathleen on what to do with the reporters, a distinguished-looking grey-haired gentleman entered the room. The nurse stepped aside as though it was Erica's doctor. He waited quietly for the chance to talk to Marina. When she said goodbye to Kathleen and replaced the phone in the cradle, she turned toward the older man.

" I'm Douglas Turner," he said. His voice was calm and clear.

" I'm the administrator of the hospital. I guess by now you are aware that the press and the media have caught on to this accident and that they are already arriving," he continued."Actually, they're a little late.

Nevertheless, they're here now," he added.

" Well, Doctor Turner -" Marina responded. "Keep them away from Erica."

" Call me Mister Turner, thank you," he replied.

" Excuse me ... Mister Turner," Marina continued. "I hope you're planning to keep them out of here?" Marina asked.

" Oh, you can be sure of that. We're not very big on having the press scurrying around the hospital. We have that problem from time to time, when they think that a celebrity from one of the casinos has been admitted. That's why I'm very surprised that they haven't been here before this. Rest assured, Mrs. Spencer, that the press won't be any bother to you. When you need to come and go, just ask the nurse at the station to show you the doctors elevator, which will take you directly to the parking garage. There, you can exit the hospital without being noticed by the press. They are huddled in the lobby and won't be expecting you to leave the building through the doctor's entrance. I'll do everything I can to protect you and Erica from them and their cameras."

*

On the day of Leslie's attack the press had been hanging around the Rutledge Place, and evening had settled in. The sun disappeared over the bay and the inland. The strong ocean breeze subsided and darkness soon followed. Jeff returned to the beach house

GULLS

from his day of golfing and dinner with drinks. He joined the foursome of golfers at the country club for an early evening of dinner and conversation. when he returned, instead of finding Leslie waiting for him, he found that the house was closed up and she was nowhere to be found.

On the table in the small kitchen was her note: " I should be back before the sun goes down. I'm going to the north end of the island for some sun. Hope you had a good golf game. See ya' later. Love, Leslie."

Jeff thought that it was strange that it was nearly dark and Leslie hadn't returned. He decided to walk to the north beach and possibly meet up with her. The beach house was only a short block from the beach, so Jeff didn't take long to arrive on the sand.

The telltale signs of the day's activity were all around him as he began walking to the north. The sand, still warm from the afternoon sun, was covered with footprints that were ever so slightly filling in with loose sand that blew across the beach. The lifeboats were pulled well up on the beach and turned upside down. The lifeguard shacks were lying on the backs so that children would not climb on them during the night. A few lingering sea gulls chased in and out of the shallow water trying to catch the last of the days small morsels that were washed ashore. A few couples walked hand in hand along the beach, and the surf was highlighted by the floodlights that were pointed toward the surf from motels and houses that lined the beach fronts.

After walking for twenty minutes, Jeff began to get

more and more concerned that he had not seen Leslie. In front of him stretched the open deserted beach. Behind him, the lights from the streets and houses on the inhabited part of the island grew smaller and smaller. The night sky began to blanket the island and a mist developed.

Occasionally, a small Jeep or four-wheel drive pick-up would pass him going to the south end of the island. These were the surf fisherman returning from the day's fishing exposition. Some would stay out all night surf-fishing. Jeff could see some of their gas lanterns in the distance. This was the only thing that broke the otherwise eerie and lonely feeling that was coming over him. Onward he walked, straining his eyes to see if someone might be walking in the opposite direction - Maybe someone returning from spending the day along the wildlife preserve part of the island, but there was no one. He continued to grow worried for her safety.

After walking for nearly an hour, Jeff considered turning around and returning to the beach house. Possibly, he thought, Leslie may have returned to the house and decided to walk to a store and do some shopping. Maybe she connected up with her sister and they went into the city. He began in his mind reasoning why she was not at the house. While looking for an explanation, Jeff didn't notice that Byron was speeding along the hard sand of the beach, close to the water, in his Jeep. Soon, the light from the vehicle reflected against the evening's damp air and Jeff turned to see it.

Just then, a red flashing light appeared on the top. It ricocheted off the damp night air. Byron turned it on just before rolling up to Jeff.

" How do?" Byron asked, as he stopped beside Jeff and turned off the Jeep. It was quiet except for the sound of the breakers as the tide moved further out.

" Not bad," Jeff replied. " I'm looking for my girlfriend. She's out here somewhere, I'm sure of it."

" What makes you think she's up here?" Byron asked.

" She said she was going to this part of the island to spend the day in the sun. It's not like her to be out here by herself for this long. So I thought I would take a walk down here and see if I could meet up with her. But no such luck," Jeff added. "I must have walked a mile or more."

" When did she come down here?" Byron quizzed.

" She left this morning. She packed a lunch, took her blanket and I haven't seen her since."

" Come on. Hop in," Byron instructed. " We'll take a ride to the end of the beach, where it meets with the bay. If she's up here, we'll be sure to find her. Unless you would like to walk the three miles down and the three miles back."

" No, thanks," Jeff replied. " I appreciate this."

Jeff grabbed the window support with his right hand and pulled himself onto the Jeep. Without delay, Byron started the engine and they were rolling along the beach. The high beams from the Jeep peered through the night and across the vacant beach in front of them. Occasionally they passed a surf fisherman standing knee-deep in the surf. The fog was beginning to close in on them.

Having driven the entire length of the north beach and back, Jeff was more than a little disappointed that they had not seen Leslie.

" Would you do me a favor?" Jeff asked Byron. "Would you drive me to my beach house. Maybe she has returned. I would like to get there as quickly as I can just in case she has gotten back and decided to go find me."

" Sure thing," Byron replied as he made a wide turn on the beach and headed back.

When they pulled up in front of the beach house, it was easy to see that Leslie had not returned. The house was dark. Jeff returned from golf before darkness set in and did not turn on any lights in the house. It was dark inside.

" I'll wait here for a while," Jeff added. " I'm sure she must be around the island somewhere. I had better stay here until she gets back."

" Okay," Byron said. " I'll check back with you later, just in case." He could see the effects of the quandary on Jeff's face.

Jeff entered the beach house and Byron stayed in the Jeep, remaining parked in front, wondering if the girl was still on the beach, wondering if something was seriously wrong.

" Base ONE, do you read me, over." Byron stated into the microphone on the Jeep radio.

" Base one here," the voice answered.

" Rick, this is Byron. I have just returned to the

inland from the north end beach. Went looking for some girl. I spotted a guy walking the beach by himself. I don't know why, but I decided to stop and ask if he needed anything. Just a gut reaction, but I had this funny feeling something was wrong."

" Well, Byron, did you find the girl?" Rick questioned.

" No, we didn't. He said she went to the north end of the island this morning to sunbathe, while he went to play golf, he said, and hasn't seen her since."

" How old is this couple?" Rick asked.

" I don't know, maybe twenty-five, maybe less. I'm no cop, ya know. I didn't ask all that many questions of him. But something doesn't feel good about it."

On the south end of the island, in front of Rutledge Place, the local television van sat waiting for instruction for their next assignment. The attempt at trying to get an interview with Marina or David had failed. Kathleen did a good job of instructing them that Mr. and Mrs. Spencer would be home shortly, but they would have to wait outside. For the last two and a half hours, they waited in the van. The police scanner positioned on the dashboard had been stopping on activated frequencies with the same short messages being transmitted, none of which were important to them. Suddenly, Byron's message to Rick was picked up by the two television technicians that were seated in the van.

" Did you hear that?" the one seated behind the steering wheel asked of the passenger.

"Yah', that's unusual." the other replied. " Who do you suppose that was?" They waited and listened intently for Byron's voice to return.

"I'm going back to the north end...maybe I'll see something," Byron said over the radio to Rick.

He decided to return to the deserted beach and drive the length of the island one more time. As he navigated the Jeep along the beach, keeping closer to the sand dunes, he couldn't help but notice the headlights in his mirror. Behind him, following almost a half mile back, was the van for WATL TV. They hugged close to the hard sand to keep the two-wheel-drive vehicle from becoming bogged down in the soft sand and bringing their expedition to an abrupt halt. Byron had no idea that they were on the same trek. Soon, additional vehicles followed. In his mirror he saw headlights from a half dozen vehicles heading his way.

The message from Byron to Rick had been listened to by almost every news reporter and radio and television reporter that had been sent to find the rest of the story. Within the next half hour, there were no less then twenty vehicles on the beach. Already, a few were stuck in the soft sand, with little left to do but to wait for a tow truck to get them out. Overhead, two television helicopters raced along the beach at the point where the breakers met with the sand. Flying extremely low, they began to criss cross the narrow island, driven to this search by a hunch and looking for anything that could develop into news. The hunt began. Byron thought that it was all ridiculous. Maybe he missed something, but where in the hell did all these people come from anyway?

" Base one, do you read, over," Byron said into the microphone.

" Go ahead, Byron," Rick's voice answered.

"What in the hell's going on out here?" Byron asked. "All of a sudden we're covered with news vans and choppers."

Byron stopped the Jeep and allowed the rest of the news seekers to catch up to him. The WATL TV van pulled along side of Byron's Jeep and the driver asked," Hey, are you the guy that is looking for the girl?"

" What makes you think I'm looking for anyone?" Byron asked.

" We overheard a conversation over the radio, picked it up from the scanner in the van. Thought it might be you looking for the girl."

Byron did not answer the two in the van. Instead, he started the engine to the Jeep and sped along the beach looking ahead in the mist to see anyone that might be walking. His headlights hit the fog in front of him and he could tell that the wall of white was closing in on him.

CHAPTER FIVE:
Skylight

Marina was convinced by Erica's doctor that she should return home and get some sleep. There wasn't anything that she could do and Erica was expected to remain stable throughout the night. After David arrived and spent some time with Erica and Marina, he and Marina left through the rear exit of the hospital and returned to the Rutledge Place.

" Good evenin', ma'am. How is Erica doin'?" Kathleen asked as she met them at the door.

" Where are all the TV and the newspaper people?"Marina asked while surprised that no one was around.

" Don't know, ma'am." Kathleen replied. " All of a suddin' they just lit out of here like there was some sort of fire somewhere."

"Well, I'm glad of that, Kathleen. Maybe we can get some sleep."

"Would you be needin' anything?" Kathleen asked.

GULLS

" No, I don't think so. I'm too tired to even think really. David, If it's all the same with you, I'll just go on to bed," Marina responded.

" I'll join you, I'm beat."

"The boy is already in bed, ma'am," Kathleen added. " Stayin in the house all day and watching out the windows must have made him tired. He was bored stiff he was."

The curtains were still opened, revealing the dimly lit beach that stretched to the ocean. Marina was too tired to bother closing them. She knew that they were controlled by computer and felt that they would probably close by themselves at sometime during the night. Inside of half an hour, she found herself lying in bed next to David. Even though she was tired, she still had trouble falling off to sleep.

The clouds slipped past the skylight and Marina watched the stars disappear and then appear again. Marina could tell by David's heavy breathing that he had already gone to sleep. Lying there, deep in thought, Marina slowly began to dose.

Perched on the top of the curtain rod near the ceiling was a single gull. It stood watching, with one foot tucked up under the downy feathers and the other claw wrapped tightly around the metal. The house was quiet. Marina turned onto her side and had a clear view of the beach and the ocean to the south. Suddenly, she heard a slight click. Slowly, the white curtains began to move across the windows. The motor that pulled them hummed. The sound came from somewhere behind the wall.

At the far end of the room, the sound of the automatic motor and the slight vibration from the rollers of the curtains alarmed the gull. No one knew the gull was there. No one knew how it managed to get into the house. It opened its eyes and was suddenly alarmed.

Placing the other foot on the rail, it looked in all directions. The dome skylight overhead became brighter as the clouds moved clear of the moon. The gull saw this as the escape. Lunging forward, it left the rail. The curtains on the north side of the house closed and the sound of the motor stopped. The gull flew across the expanse of the room and then back to its perch.

"David, wake up ! David, did you hear something? David, wake up ! Listen !" Marina pleaded.

The gull flew up into the fifteen-foot dome skylight and abruptly struck the tempered glass. It fell past the suspended bedroom where Marina and David were sleeping and landed on top of the sculpture of gulls in the living room below.

" Wake up, damn it, David !" Marina said as she poked her hand into his side.

" What. What is it?" he responded still half asleep.

" There's something in here. I think there's a damned gull in here."

" Don't be silly. It's in your mind," he answered. "You're having a nightmare."

Just then, the gull took to the air again, letting out a screech that could be heard throughout the house.

" I told you," Marina yelled as she raised up from the

bed on her elbows.

" Oh, shit," David was quick to respond.

The gull continued its relentless attempts at getting out of the house. It flew from one window to another. David got out of bed and headed directly for the stairs. Marina grabbed the blanket and pulled it tightly around her body, being careful to leave enough loose so that she could pull the blanket over her head.

" Kill it ! Kill it, David," she screamed.

David went down to the controls for the curtains and the lights. Not knowing exactly how to operate the system, he mistakenly pressed the key to open all the curtains and to turn on all the indirect lighting, both inside and outside of the house. The gull appeared to be startled by it all and increased the screams and flying attempts to get out. No matter what keys David pressed, nothing responded to his efforts. Looking up to the skylight, he watched the gull make its unsuccessful attempts to exit through the dome skylight. Each time it would hit the glass and then return to the other side of the room screeching on the way.

" Kill it ! Get it out of here !" Marina cried out.

Just then, Kathleen and Christopher appeared in the living room. Awakened and startled by Marina's screaming, they ran from the back rooms on the first level. The gull swooped across the room and darted toward David. Shielding his face from the oncoming predator, he ran toward the steps and for cover under the stairway.

" My god," Kathleen gasped. " How did he get in here?"

" Don't know," David said.

"Watch out !" Chris, yelled out as the gull swooped again in the direction of Kathleen.

" Kill it. Please, kill it," Marina continued to scream.

David stood for a minute looking around the room. He noticed a gun cabinet in the hall. There were a half dozen or more rifles behind the glass door.

Outside the house, the beach was deserted. The clouds that were moving across the island had now moved out to sea and the moonlight illuminated the Rutledge Place against the night sky. The dome skylight was brightly lit from the lights inside the house. Like a beacon it could be seen from almost all points of the beach. Inside, the screaming from Marina continued. David knew he would have to do something fast.

He made his way to the gun cabinet. Opening the glass door, he found an old, single shot twelve-gauge shotgun. Directly below the glass door was a drawer and inside there were boxes of bullets. Carefully, he looked through the boxes and then stopped on the box marked "twelve gauge magnum."

In the bedroom, Marina was crying uncontrollably. Scared to leave the shelter of the bed and the blankets, she pulled a fist full of blanket to her face and buried her nose and mouth into it. Peering over her fists, she watched as the gull continued to fly back and forth across the room. Occasionally, it darted up to the dome skylight and then, as though in anger, it swooped down to the living room. Each time in its attempt, it would come dangerously close to Kathleen and Chris.

GULLS

" I've got you now, you sorry son of a bitch," David said to himself as he placed a single shell into the chamber of the shotgun.

Using both hands, he closed the breech of the gun and headed for the steps. From where Kathleen and Chris were crouched, they couldn't see David as he started up the stairs to the bedroom level. The gull never stopped flying back and forth across the room.

" I'll get him," David said as he got to the top of the stairs.

" Kill it !" Marina yelled again.

The gull swooped back and forth below the suspended bedroom. David knew he would have to wait for it to fly up to the skylight, in order to get a good shot at it.

" Come on, you bastard," David said.

As though responding to command, the gull swooped upward into the domed skylight. David moved to the front of the bedroom. Pushing the telescope aside knocking it over. He made his way so that he was close to being directly under the dome. The gull remained in the skylight, continuing the horrifying screams. David lifted the gun to his cheek. It was then that he became visible to Kathleen and Christopher.

" No !" Kathleen screamed from the first floor suddenly realizing what David was about to do.

" Kill it !" Marina cried out in desperation.

Carefully and deliberately David sighted in on the gull. He pulled the metal comma-shaped trigger to his thumb. The firing pin slammed against the shell, and the gun-powder erupted with a tremendous bang. More then a hundred pellets rushed through the barrel headed in the direction of the gull. The sound deafened everyone. The gull continued striking the sphere of glass with its beak as the pellets being sent through the air widened their path.

" Dear Lord above," Kathleen said as the gun went off.

The pellets struck the glass dome with colossal force. Instantly, the hand blown tempered glass sphere erupted into a million tiny pieces, and began the descent to the floor thirty six feet below. David stood watching as the glass fell like heavy rain-drops from a rain storm. As they passed the bedroom level, the organized shape of broken glass remained shaped as a sphere. Soon, gravity and speed took over, and the shape distorted as the pieces raced each other to the marble floor below.

Looking upward, David watched the gull depart from the opening in the ceiling. He had escaped the pellets. By sheer luck, the lead struck the glass at one end and caused the sphere to break and released the gull from the dome. It flew away unharmed.

The slivers of glass finally struck the floor and scattered in all directions. Fortunately, the tempered glass didn't cut either Kathleen or Christopher as they came at them flying in all directions. The last pieces came to a stop and the sound of glass chips bouncing on the marble floor came to a halt. David stood staring out the fifteen-foot hole in the ceiling, at the night sky. The coolness of the night air rushed through the opening and across the bed where Marina remained sobbing. Kathleen and Christopher stood from their crouched position in the living room. The pieces of glass covered everything like remnants of a hail storm.

Suddenly, the mantle clock began to chime the Westminster Chime, and the motor driven curtains began to move from the corners of the room. Soon, the Rutledge Place would be enshrouded in the curtains of white fabric. Marina could no longer see the beach or the ocean. She continued to look toward the night sky through the opening in the ceiling.

" Please. Please, leave us alone," she sobbed.

CHAPTER SIX:

Boom-Box

Darkness enveloped the north end of the island. Byron continued to drive his Jeep up and down the beach in hopes of finding the girl that he was sure was more than lost or delayed. Deep in the pit of his stomach, he felt the burning and heavy sensation that something was drastically wrong.

The headlights from the others that were now looking for Leslie appeared in all directions along the deserted beach. Two news helicopters criss crossed above the fog and over the north end in hopes that they might spot something. The bayberry bushes that covered the north end of the island were thick. There was no way that they could spot anything from the air. After more than three hours of searching, they gave up. Because this wasn't an official search from the island police, the search ended early.

One by one the vans and the four-wheel-drive vehicles left the beach. Byron parked his Jeep on top of a sand dune and waited. Having turned off the engine, he sat in the Jeep watching the other vehicles as they left the beach. Soon there was no one there and the beach was quiet again.

" Base, this is unit one, do you read me, over," he called into the microphone.

" Unit one, go ahead," the voice of his partner replied.

" They've given up on their search, Rick."

" You heading back to base?" Rick asked.

" Shortly," Byron said.

Byron put one foot up onto the dash-board of the Jeep. Carefully, he placed the microphone back into the slot under the dash. As he stared out toward the ocean, his thoughts were on the missing girl. In his mind, he thought that he might be overreacting. After all, she hadn't really been gone all that long. But something in the timing and the fact that she had planned to spend the afternoon, or rather the whole day in the sun, told Byron that she should have been back at the beach house. He knew that most people returned to their houses before the sun went down. Maybe she drowned out here, he thought.

The air was still. The sound of the ocean was more than a hundred yards from Byron somewhere in the fog. He thought he heard something. Shortly, after listening real hard, he was sure that he heard something. It sounded like a voice in the distance. He looked down at the radio in the Jeep to see if it was on. It was not. He reached down and turned off the two way radio to be sure. He still heard the voice. Stepping out of the Jeep, he decided to walk a few feet along the top of the sand dunes to see if he could still hear the voice. He did.

" You can say all you want about Casino gambling but it hasn't helped the school board or education all that much, at least not hear in Atlantic City," the voice said. Byron heard the voice clearly. He was certain it wasn't his imagination.

I'll be damned, Byron said to himself. Somewhere, down in the bayberry bushes on the other side of the sand dunes, was a radio. The voice he heard was coming from a radio - he was sure of it.

" Anybody there?" he called out.

" We'll be back to discuss the effects of gambling on the poor, after we take the time for these important commercial messages," the radio announcer said.

Byron heard it loud and clear, although the radio wasn't turned on all that loud. Returning to the Jeep, he reached in and grabbed the flashlight that was fastened to the side of the seat. The light was powerful. When he turned in the direction of the sound, the light peered through the night mist and looked like an alien searchlight in a desperate attempt to locate life forms.

" Anyone there?" he called again.

Byron shined the light toward the same place that he had heard the radio so clearly. Walking sideways down a sand dune, he continued toward the sound of music.

" ... come see the softer side of Sears," the song went. It was a radio commercial.

GULLS

Sweeping the light back and forth along the sand, Byron searched for the radio. As he pushed his way through some branches, he came upon it. It was not very loud, but in the stillness of the summer night, it did seem louder than it had for Leslie. Byron squinted his eyes at the blanket twisted up on the sand. He saw the dark stains of blood on it and on the sand leading under the bushes. He continued to scan the area with the flashlight. Finding the cooler, he opened it. There were still the remains of ice cubes scattered on top of the sandwiches. Now they appeared like small highly polished pebbles rather than defined cubes. He knew that nothing was used from the cooler. It was still full. Leslie's bathing suit and running shorts were lying in the sand. Side by side were her running shoes. Just then, he noticed the trail of blood stains that led under the bayberry bushes.

He began crawling along the ground, with the flashlight in his right hand, peering under the branches for Leslie. The branches snagged on his clothing. With the light as an aid, he looked closely at the sand and the marks from Leslie crawling in her desperate attempt to flee from the attacking gulls. Byron stopped, looking directly below him in the sand, he saw the clear footprints made by the gulls. The pattern was such that they were moving forward and then in circles, and then forward again. He was sure this was the pattern of gulls that were aggressively attacking Leslie. The blood stains in the sand became larger and larger and actually formed clusters. He could tell that the injured and bleeding person was moving more slowly and the blood drops got larger.

It appeared to Byron that he had gone along the sand under the bushes for a mile. He stopped again. Again, he studied the sand with the light.

" Oh, shit !" he said in a whisper.

There was no mistaking the signs of sand crabs and their sideways walking in the sand. Hundreds of prints in the soft sand showed Byron the way. They were all heading in the same direction. Soon, the prints blended with those of the gulls, and Byron knew it wouldn't be too far. Lifting the light as high as he could over his head, he directed it through the branches. There, no more than ten feet in front of him, he could see the body. He could see the body of a completely naked woman.

" What the ...?" he said out loud.

Leslie's body was lying face down in the sand. Her thighs and her back was covered with sand crabs. He could hear the sounds they made. It sounded to him, like breakfast cereal soon after its covered with cold milk. Her arms were stretched out in front of her, showing her hopeless attempt at escaping. Byron let his face fall into the sand and his arm fell with the flashlight. Uncontrollably, he began heaving every-thing from the bottom of his stomach. Coughing and gagging, he turned back toward the tracks in the sand that he had just made and crawled more than one hundred yards to the starting point of the ordeal.

✳

On the residential section of the beach, far south from the area where Byron had found the body, Jeff returned. He had waited as long as he could and he was convinced that there was something drastically wrong. He would walk the beach all night long if necessary, in hopes of finding Leslie.

He came upon a form of a woman walking in the opposite direction. The body motion from the distance looked exactly like Leslie's. Jeff strained his eyes hard. He then began to walk even faster.

" Leslie," he yelled into the misty night air.

" Leslie, is that you?"

" Jeff. Jeff. Jeff," the voice answered.

Instantly, he broke into a run. But the other person did not. Arriving in front of the girl, he asked in a panic.

" Leslie, where have you been?"

" I'm not Leslie, Jeff. You still can't tell us apart can you?" Tonya replied. "I saw your note on the door...where's Leslie?"

With that reply, Jeff couldn't stand it any longer. Stretching out his arms to hold Tonya, he broke into tears. Jeff was sure that something was wrong, that something had happened to Leslie.

" My God, what's wrong?" Tonya asked, while entering into Jeff's embrace.

"Something has happened to Leslie. I'm sure of it,"he sobbed.

CHAPTER SEVEN:

Under the Bushes

By the time that Byron had reached the Jeep he was sure that he had seen the most grotesque thing. He was also certain that by the time the night was over, he would see it again. While reaching for the microphone in the Jeep, he took a deep breath trying again not to throw up. Acid from deep within his stomach moved up his throat and stopped at his vocal chords.

" Base, this is unit one."

" Go ahead, Byron."

" I found her, down here in the bayberry bushes. It's not very pretty. She's dead."

" Where did you say you are?"

" About a mile up on the north end. I'm parked on the top of the dunes. Go ahead and call the coroner or the ambulance ...whoever."

" Okay. Stay put. I'll get them down there,"Rick instructed.

Byron sat in the Jeep still in bewilderment that sea

gulls could do such a thing. In his mind he saw again the tracks from the attackers. He knew all too well that the pursuit of Leslie had been relentless. He could still see the prints in the sand from the gulls circling and then moving in on the victim again and again. He tried to imagine himself wanting to escape the birds and like Leslie, trying to crawl under the bushes, through the thick and jagged branches. He realized her dilemma and could feel the frustration and the pain that she must have gone through.

His thoughts were broken when he heard the oncoming brigade of police and emergency vehicles long before he could see them. Soon, the flashing lights they were using caused the misty air to flash like fireworks in multi-colors. There were so many sirens being used that the sound meshed together as some sort of synthesized out-of-tune chorus. It all added to the already eerie and tragic night.

The vehicles that could drive in the soft sand, pulled close to Byron and his Jeep. Others waited on the hard sandy surface closer to the water.

" She's down there. About a hundred yards under the bushes."

" You goin' with us?" the tall police officer asked as he started down the sand dune.

" No. I'll stay here and wait. Just follow the tracks in the sand. You can't miss her."

The network vans and the local newspaper reporters parked their vehicles by the water and walked up on the beach with their cameras and hand-held spotlights blazing into the night mist. After ten minutes or so, the policeman returned from under the bushes.

" God damn. I've never seen anything like that," he said.

" How you going to get her out of there?" Byron asked.

" Don't know. We'll have to pull her out somehow."

" How about a winch?" the other cop said.

" Yep. That'll work. Call Scott, he's on duty tonight, I think?"

He was referring to Scott Hamner, from "Hamner's Texaco." The night on-call duty for the towing was Scott's. No doubt, he
was listening to his scanner and had heard the call for the emergency equipment.

" He's down here," someone said from the background.

" Get him up here," the cop said.

Another cop walked up to Byron, he had under his arm, a body bag. Byron remembered seeing one of those bags at a traffic accident on the island. He knew instantly what it was that the officer had under his arm.

" Who's goin' in after her?" the cop asked.

" I'll go," Byron offered. Although, he wasn't thrilled with the idea, for some reason he instinctively responded with the offer.

" Wait for Scott."

Soon, the tow truck backed up to the sand dunes and Scott turned the spot light on in the rear of the tow truck. Byron heard the sound of the towing cable as Scott pulled it from the rear of the truck. The whining of the steel cable as it was pulled through the metal eye, put a chill up Byron's' back. He wouldn't normally react to the sound, however, given what they were about to do, the sound seemed to be more amplified.

" Here. Pull this along with you."

Byron still couldn't believe that this was the way they were going to get Leslie out from under the bushes.

" Just hook the cable around the feet, wrap it a few times. Be careful and get some sort of knot around her ankles. It'll be hard because this stuff is heavy, but if you grab it here and pull hard, it will get tight enough. When we begin to pull her out, it will automatically pull tighter. Call out to me and I'll pull her through the sand." Scott instructed.

Byron listened carefully to the instructions from Scott. He took a deep breath again.

" You ready," he asked knowing what he was about to see again under the bushes.

" Let's do it," the young officer replied.

Jeff and Tonya heard the commotion from the beach at the south end. Automatically, they assumed that it had something to do with Leslie, and they began running as fast as they could toward the flashing lights. Side by side they ran along the beach. Occasionally, they would splash in the shallow salt water as it slid up the beach with the incoming tide. Arriving at the assortment of vehicles with flashing lights, they slowed to a walk.

" What's goin' on?" Jeff asked.

" Some girl. They found some girl," somebody answered.

" Where?"

" In the bushes. She's dead. They're pulling her out now."

" No !" Tonya cried out, as she made her way toward the sand dunes.

Just then, a cop stepped out from the crowd of on-lookers and grabbed Tonya.

" Wait here," he said to her as he held her arm.

" No. No. It's Leslie. I know it is,"Tonya cried out as her eyes filled with tears.

Jeff went past Tonya and weaved his way through the people and the commotion to the top of the sand dune. The sound of the steel cable had stopped. They all waited for the signal from Byron and the police officer to begin pulling the body from under the branches.

" Quiet ! Quiet, damn it !" someone yelled.

Everyone stopped talking immediately. The sounds of police radio transmissions was the only thing that could be heard. The coroner stood atop the dune star-ing out into the night air. He waited like the grim reaper for the body to be presented to him.

" Okay !" someone yelled. " They said go ahead."

Just then, Scott pushed the lever down and the sound of the winch motor could be heard by every-one. Under the bayberry bushes,Byron had success-fully rolled Leslie's dead weight body into the plastic bag and with the help of the cop, they maneuvered the body under the thick branches and into the bag. She was face down. Byron was sure that there were probably sand crabs inside the bag along with the body, but couldn't bring himself to take his powerful flashlight and search the inside before zipping it closed. Carefully wrapping the cable around Leslie's ankles, Byron fashioned a loose knot to hold her with the cable. After they yelled to the crowd to go ahead, they rolled slightly away from the body.

The cracking sounds of branches being broken was the first thing they both heard. It sounded like someone braking kindling. The cable vanished under the sand on the top of the dune where the people were standing as the tension was applied to the cable. Then, the cable lifted into the air as it became more and more taunt. Suddenly, the plastic bag began to move along the sand. Byron watched as the weight of Leslie's body formed a trench through the sand as it was being pulled along, erasing the tracks made by the gulls and erasing Byron's crawling patterns in his trek to find her. They both stayed speechless as the body slowly was pulled into the darkness under the branches. They were in no hurry to follow. Instead, they waited for a minute or two.

" Oh my God. Oh my God," Tonya cried out when the body-bag appeared in front of her and Jeff.

Jeff watched as the body bag slowly came into view from under the bushes. The sand was being plowed up by the weight of it and as it was being dragged closer to the sand dunes.

" Stop," someone called out.

Scott was talking with someone as he stood by the controls of the truck. The lever was pushed down and the winch motor continued pulling in the cable.

" Stop ! Damn it !" the voice yelled again.

By the time Scott reacted to the command, the bag had been pulled halfway up the sand dune. A pile of dry sand had been pushed up. Behind the bag, a smooth path was made by the passing of Leslie's heavy body.

" I wanna see her," Tonya said through her sobbing.

Jeff grabbed Tonya around the shoulders, and tried to convince her that she shouldn't.

" Who are you?" the coroner asked as he approached Tonya and Jeff from somewhere in the darkness.

" I think I ... I'm her sister."

" Ma'am, I don't think you should now. Maybe later, in town."

" No. I want to see her now," Tonya demanded.

The coroner looked around for someone with a flashlight that he could borrow.

" Let me have that ?" the coroner asked, as he grabbed for the high powered flashlight from one of the police.

He turned the light down onto the body bag and crouched to open the zipper. Holding the flashlight tightly under his armpit and aiming it at the bag, he carefully pushed the sand away from the zipper before starting.

" Tonya, why don't you wait. You can't. You can't do this to yourself," Jeff pleaded.

GULLS

Through her sobbing Tonya continued begging, "Let me see her, I want to be sure."

Just then, Byron came crawling out from under the branches.

" I wouldn't do that. Don't open it," he said.

" I don't care. Open it," Tonya screamed.

The coroner began pulling the zipper along the enshrouded torso, with the light still under his arm shining the way. As he pulled the zipper past Leslie's shoulders and began moving it down the center of her back, the first sand crab appeared from under the plastic and scurried into the darkness. Tonya shivered and screamed at the sight of it. Additional crabs were still gripping Leslie's skin and the points of her open wounds, they were reluctant to leave as the coroner's light shined on them.

" Please, Tonya, not now," Jeff pleaded.

Tonya didn't say any more, she just stood sobbing into her hands waiting for the coroner to finish. Soon, the bag was opened along Leslie's body revealing her buttocks. Tonya and Jeff saw the two indentations just past the base of her bloodied back. Tonya was first to recognize the dimples that separated the two of them from being identical twins.

" Oh my God ! Leslie !" she cried out.

The coroner began to signal for help to turn the lifeless body over, so that Tonya could see her sister.

" No. That's all," Jeff said. Tonya buried her head into Jeff's chest and continued crying.

" It's my fault. It's my fault," she cried. "If I hadn't been here. I shouldn't have come here."

As Jeff held Tonya close and sank his face into her hair, he could hear the zipper of the body bag being pulled again along Leslie's body as the coroner closed the bag. He knew that she was being sealed in darkness in the plastic cocoon. He knew right then that he would never see her again. He too began sobbing.

By the time the other policeman crawled from under the bushes, Leslie was placed into the coroner's Jeep Wagoneer and people were being asked to leave the beach. Tonya and Jeff were taken into a police car and they were waiting for the cop to return them to the south end of the island. The investigation would begin with the autopsy.

✳

CHAPTER EIGHT:
Buried in the Sand

By ten a.m., the beaches were lined with signs reading, "Please, DO NOT feed the gulls". Island officials weren't sure if the tactic would work, but felt it might be worth the try. Radio and television news had been reporting on sporadic incidents of gull attacks on beaches and lakes throughout the U.S. The reports of attacks on vacationers had put an immediate damper on the amount of people vacationing on the beaches. Summer home rentals were down for the upcoming Labor Day weekend as more and more cancellations happened.

Brigantine Island beach officials, the head of the beach patrol, the mayor of the city and the Chief of Police devised a plan. As the sun began to appear from the east, heavy equipment was positioned at the south end of the island. Four huge yellow scrappers were lined up and ready to push the sand and level it. In front of them, four pieces of heavy equipment used for scooping up sand and sifting out the shells faced to the north beaches. They lead the way, gathering the clam shells that the nights tide had brought up on shore. The scrappers followed and made certain that the beach was leveled. By the time the eight pieces of equipment made their way from one end of the island beaches to the other, they left behind them a smooth, level, and clean beach. Inside the four lead sifters, were more than twenty tons of clam shells.

Dark gray smoke poured from the stacks of the equipment as they began the slow and meticulous journey across the sands. Bill King stood on top of a sand dune watching the expedition. As the equipment approached him from the south, he watched the hundreds of gulls gathering behind them. This would surely lure every gull on the island to the empty north beach. The plan would be to dump the shells on the bay side of the island and keep the gulls there. The feeding frenzy would keep them off the south beaches and prevent people from feeding them.

By the time that the first of the day's sun worshippers had arrived on the beach, the gulls were nowhere to be found. By the thousands, they stayed at the mountain of shells. A bulldozer and the driver were positioned close by. Occasionally, he would push the mountain of shells, uncovering a fresh supply for the feeding scavengers.

By noon, officials felt that the situation was under control. Lifeguards could return to the duties of watching the bathers in the water. They could even take some time to watch the "babes." The only waterfowl on the beach were sandpipers scurrying up to the incoming tide, only to turn and run from the salty water as it chased them back to the sloping beach. An occasional gull would fly over the breakers as it made its way to the north end of the island to join the others.

Perched in his beach chair was fifty-six-year old Don Dalasandro. On his right side, he positioned his bright red cooler filled with the cold drinks for the day. On his left, he planted his beach umbrella deep in the sand. It would provide the shade to protect him from the afternoon's strong sun. Strung around his neck was his most important item for the days activity - his high-powered binoculars. From his vantage point, he would be able to view clearly anyone walking the beach. As the young girls passed him, he took full advantage of watching their every motion as they "strut their stuff".

Also on the beach, was the Nicoll family. Every year, they would take a vacation, renting the same beach house to spend one week enjoying the residential island with its peaceful serenity. This year was no different. Warren Nicoll was peacefully reading his Sports Illustrated magazine, listing the upcoming seasons predictions for the National Football League. His two boys were busily digging in the sand. It amazed Warren's wife that the boys had not gone near the water all day. Instead, they dug the most impressive hole in the sand. The two foot deep, three foot wide and six feet long trench was being fashioned for Warren.

" C'mon, Dad," the one boy beckoned, as he pulled

on Warren's arm to join in on their fun." C'mon, let us bury you in the sand."

" So, that's what you've been doing all afternoon?"

" C'mon" the other son repeated, while pulling on the other arm.

" Oh, go ahead, Warren," his wife added. " The boys worked hard to dig that hole."

" Well, it did keep them quiet for the day, didn't it? Oh, I suppose so," Warren said as he raised from the beach chair.

Within minutes, they had Warren buried under a mound of sand. It felt cool to his body, but he could also feel the weight of it. That was something that he would never had guessed. He was careful to move his body slightly as they dumped the cool damp sand around him, filling the tomb. Before long, they had buried all but his head under the granules. Once they were finished, they had gathered behind him, and plotted his afternoon's demise - all in good fun.

" Well, dear, the boys and myself are hungry. We are going to the beach house for lunch. Can we bring you anything?" she asked.

" Oh, c'mon, give me a break. You're not going to leave me here, are you?"

" Yea, we are." one boy added.

" Let me out of here," Warren pleaded.

" Warren, it'll be all right," his wife told him, as she placed a ball cap on top of his head.

Next, she propped a blanket behind his head so that he would be more comfortable. Taking some sun-screen from the plastic squeeze bottle, she carefully put some on his nose and cheeks with her index and second finger.

" The boys are just having fun. Don't worry," she told him as she anointed his face with the lotion.

" Oh, this is great. C'mon, let me up from here," he pleaded again.

The two boys continued their laughing while they carefully patted the sand neatly around their father's body.

" We'll be back in twenty minutes," she said, " It won't kill you and they'll have a few good laughs."

She knelt in the sand and kissed Warren on the forehead.

" Okay, but no more than twenty minutes. Promise?"

" We promise !" the boys added.

Warren lay in the sand peering forward at the rest of the beach in front of him and out to the ocean.

No more than thirty feet in front of him and slightly to the left was Don Dalasandro with his binoculars. On the other side, a young couple, little more than teenagers, lay on their blanket listening to rap music on the radio. Warren found it a little more than irritating. He watched as the man in the beach chair lifted the big black binoculars to his face every time a girl or woman approached from either side of the beach. He fixed on them until they passed in front of him, and then stayed with them as they continued down the beach. The modern fashions for bathing suits revealed a lot more than they did when he was younger. So, he found the view through his lenses most interesting and "girl watching" became his favorite vacation sport.

Warren watched, as Dalasandro raised from the beach chair with the binoculars still pressed to his face. This time, however, there were no girls in his view. He fixed on something beyond the breakers, out a long way in the Atlantic. He chewed on the cigar that he had stuffed in the corner of his mouth, and made his way across the soft sand to the hardened sand closer to the water. There he stood in his cut-off shorts, beer gut hanging over the waist band, puffing on his cigar, and staring through the looking glasses out at the ocean. While the cold Atlantic water slipped up across the sand and rushed over his feet, Don Dalasandro muttered, "Would you look at that."

A few hundred yards from the beach and directly off shore from him, Don watched the vintage Cris Craft fishing boat, bob and sway in the ocean, just beyond the incoming tide. He stood, watching through the glasses and ever so slightly adjusting the lenses to get better focused. The boat was covered with gulls. They were perched everywhere. Don squinted his eyes in disbelief. Almost every available inch of exposed boat had a gull standing on it.

Lyle Steele and his long-time companion Robert Lance, had done it again. Both consumed all the beer on board the boat and Robert had long since passed out, after heaving his guts out. He was now lying on the deck in a fetal position and had fallen off to sleep. Lyle sat propped against the engine compartment on his lawn chair. He had modified the chair so that it was partially reclined. With a little help from his feet against the side rail of the old Cris Craft, Lyle could balance himself in the perfect position, where he was most comfortable. It was in that position that he fell asleep. With his chin resting on his chest, his hands wrapped loosely around his fishing rod, and his legs slightly bent, Lyle slept quietly and comfortably through the night. The engine of the craft had belched its last breath and the cylinders soon came to a complete stop. The boat was now rocking in a gentle motion that added to the restful atmosphere and had the two of them sleeping like babies.

Gathering overhead, the gulls swarmed and circled the boat. In their sleeping state, neither noticed the sounds of the gulls nor the sounds of their wings flapping as they hovered overhead. Suddenly, a large gull dove at Lyle and struck him on the top of the head.

" God damn it, Bob, knock it off," he mumbled.

Just then, another gull moved in and struck his neck with its beak. As Lyle awoke, he could see the red inside of the gull's mouth as it pulled away from him. Instinctively, he took a swipe at the bird. Without hesitation, the gulls began to dive at him. In a reflex motion, he dropped his feet from the rail and becoming conscious, swung his arms to try and hit something. He saw the hundreds of sea gulls circling overhead.

" Jesus H. Christ," he exclaimed. " Bob,where are you?"

Lyle had no time to look for his friend. Instead, he thought of taking cover in the cabin. Shielding his face by placing his hand around the back of his neck and then having his arm folded against the side of his head, he tried to make a run for the cabin. Gulls were now all around him. Tripping over both the gulls, the empty beer cans, and the styrofoam cooler, Lyle fell to the deck. As he scrambled around the painted deck of their fishing boat, slipping on the wet surface, he found his fishing partner lying there. By now, the gulls had covered them both. Neither would survive the ordeal.

Don Dalasandro wished that his binoculars were stronger. He couldn't help but think that something serious had happened on board the wooden craft that bobbed in the water just beyond the breakers. He decided to walk over to the lifeguard stand and ask them if they had noticed the boat and the gulls. Keeping the binoculars up to his face, he walked through the shallow water in the direction of the guards, splashing along the way. For no apparent reason, the gulls suddenly lifted from the boat. Their wings stretched open and struggling to get airborne, they flapped at random.

" Oh shit !" Dalasandro said as he dropped the glasses down from his face and began to run in the direction of the stand.

Warren watched the birds fly up from the boat. It had drifted even closer to the beach. The gulls lifted in flight. Everyone looking in the direction of the ocean noticed the display of white wings as they glittered over the slate blue-gray water and the birds left the wooden vessel. They were now headed in the direction of the beach. Warren's two boys had returned from having their lunch. Each had with them, a plastic pail. They had filled the pails with water, and were now sneaking up on him from behind. Warren's eyes were glued on the approaching gulls. Panic began to set in on the beach, as people stood watching the flock. The boys never noticed the activity on the beach as they approached their father from behind.

Much to everyone's surprise, the gulls passed overhead and headed for the exposed face and head that appeared mounted on the beach. Soon, Warren realized the creatures were coming toward him. Struggling to free himself from the sand, he tightened his muscles and then pushed against the blanket of sand. His repeated attempts failed, as the gulls drew closer and closer.

" Shhhh..." the one boy gestured to his brother as they crept steadily closer to their father from behind. Crouched down, they walked in exaggerated motion, as they came up on Warren from both sides.

" Now !" the one screamed to the other, as they threw the cold water on their father. The water splashed his face from both sides, knocking off his ball cap. Not more than twenty feet in front of him, the gulls approached. Then, as though waved-off, they scattered in all directions away from him and off the beach. At first Warren was blinded from the cold water but then he could see clearly as the gulls flapped their wings and climbed higher into the clear blue sky. People on the beach scattered in all directions as the gulls did the same.

GULLS

Mike Vance watched as the Cris Craft rocked in the water just beyond the breakers.

" It's getting closer. But, I don't see anybody on it," he said.

Straining his eyes in the binoculars he tried to see some sign of life. The boat sat in the water just beyond the breakers, rocking back and forth.

" There's no fishing line over the side," he said to his partner. " I'm going out there to have a look!"

Mike jumped down from the lifeguard stand and ran over to the lifeboat. With his partners help, he pushed the life-boat into the shallow salt water. As soon as it reached deep enough water, he jumped in and placed the oars over the side. Pulling against the force of the incoming tide and fighting to get the boat over the breakers, Mike pulled with all his might. Eventually, the lifeboat settled into the deeper water and he could turn it toward the Cris Craft by pulling hard with one oar. Bathers gathered along the beach as they noticed Mike's approaching the seemingly empty vessel.

As he got closer to the stranded craft he carefully positioned the lifeboat along side. He threw a life-preserver onto the deck of the Cris Craft which got caught on the engine compartment. He pulled his lifeboat closer until it came to rest against the boat. Mike stretched his body to see into it, looking for any sign of life.

Lying on the wet deck was Lyle Steele and his friend Robert Lance. Both bodies were lifeless. Mike held the side of the Cris Craft and hurdled over the side and into it. He slid on the slippery deck and fell on his hip. Resting on one side of his body and holding onto the side of the boat, Mike viewed the morbid scene. In front of him he could see the dead corpse of Lyle Steele. Bloody salt water slid back and forth across the deck as the boat rocked with each wave. Minnows, fish heads and dead squid from the overturned bait bucket, slid along with the water and up against Mike and then over against the dead bodies. Roberts shirt was open, exposing the punctured skin for Mike to see. The gulls had torn the flesh from his arms and shoulders and his blood had saturated his shirt and pants. Just before Mike lifted himself over the side to throw up, he got a full view of Robert's face as it turned toward him with the rolling of the boat. Blood soaked his blonde hair and his skin was ripped from his forehead and cheeks. Strands of ripped flesh dangled from the skull. At the ends of each strand was a gathering of green-head flies. His sun-glasses were still on and Mike could see that the skin under the edges of his sun-glasses was still intact.

After barfing into the lifeboat that was against the Cris Craft, Mike carefully edged himself along the side of the boat until he could see Lyle Steele more closely. In Lyle's right hand Mike saw a dead gull. Lyle's grip was still tight around the bird. The gulls head was sliding back and forth in the shallow water with the motion of the boat, and Mike could see that its neck must have been broken for it to move so freely. Lyle's fingers and arms were chewed up from the attack. The gulls had pulled his shirt from him in long strips. He was face down in the bait water that saturated his pants. Mike suddenly heard the sound of a Coast Guard helicopter flying low along the beach and heading in the direction of the Cris Craft. He couldn't keep his eyes off the two men and he never looked in the direction of the helicopter. It was almost as though he couldn't raise himself up from the deck. Instead, he crouched against the side of the boat and gripped the rail tightly.

Police and rescue vehicles joined the bathers on the beach and two more lifeboats were headed in Mike's direction from both sides. Soon the helicopter hovered directly over the Cris Craft and someone joined Mike in the boat after being lowered. The rotor wash from the hovering craft picked up some of the cool water from the waves and blew it into the floundering boat and into Mike's face. It was enough to snap him out of the trance that he entered.

" You all right?" the rescuer yelled.

Mike looked at him without saying anything.

" Are you Okay?" he asked again.

" Yah, I'm Okay," Mike yelled back at him.

The sound of the rotor blades and the sound of the jet engine made it hard to hear anything. The man waved the helicopter to pull away, and the hoist was quick to be raised. Quickly, the helicopter moved away and then proceeded toward the beach. It landed on the edge of the water and remained there with the engine screaming and the rotor blades turning.

The other lifeguards had taken Mike with them and they returned to the beach and the gallery of on-lookers. The Coast Guard brought out a large boat and towed the Cris Craft to their station in Atlantic City. Lyle and Robert remained on the deck for the journey to the station. Soon, the helicopter departed from the beach and eventually, the bathers scattered to their beach blankets and chairs and people returned to the water to swim and play in the surf.

*

CHAPTER NINE:
The Concert

" For no apparent reason, gulls throughout the United States, on some of the most popular beaches, have been attacking vacationers," the announcer said. "Although, no reason has been found for the attacks, some officials have claimed that the gulls are spoiled. That they have been fed too much by vacationers and now have taken to aggressiveness in getting food. Many of the coasts more popular resorts have all but closed due to the panic created by the gulls. It's the birds all over again said one vacationer in Massachusetts."

" Please, turn it off," Marina asked.

Erica, lay in the hospital getting better each day. The rest of the family tried to somewhat enjoy the beach house.

" We now take you to Long Island and to Ronald Williams who has an extended report from one of the most ...."

GULLS

David pressed the button on the remote control and the picture on the TV went black. In the living room, Chris stood under the boarded up opening where there was once a glass dome.

" They won't get in, will they?" he asked.

" No, Chris, they won't."

" Why are they attacking everyone, why don't they leave us alone?"

Marina went to the living room and took Chris into her arms.

" I don't know, David, but we'll be leaving this place just as soon as Erica can go."

David was sure that if he didn't find something for Marina to do, that she would go crazy. Each day she went to the hospital with him to see Erica, but they would return to the Rutledge Place and she would spend the rest of the time worrying.

Ceaser's Palace offered some tickets to David's company to be used as a door prize at a luncheon. David was glad to have won the two tickets to a concert. He felt sure that this was what Marina would need to take her mind off Erica. By now, Doctor White assured them that Erica would be fine. Her wounds were healing nicely and the infection from the gull bites was under control. If all went well in the next couple of days, he would release Erica from the hospital.

" But, it will be good for you to get out of here," David pleaded with Marina. " My God, we haven't done anything since the attack. It'll be good for both of us. Wear that new green dress that you bought and let's just have a good dinner and take in the concert."

"Oh, all right. I guess it can't hurt."

By seven that evening they were dressed and ready to go. As David backed the car from the house, Marina watched for gulls on the beach. There were none. The early evening sky was beginning to turn color and the smell of salt air filled her head as she pushed the button on the door panel to close the window. Even then, she felt uncomfortable leaving Chris at the Rutledge Place for the evening. Kathleen and Chris stood at the glass window waving goodbye to them as they drove away.

" Please, no radio tonight," she asked.

David reached down and turned off the radio and they sat quietly in their thoughts as they left Brigantine Island.

" Look. There, look at them,"

High over the Casino Hotel at the other end of the bridge from the island, they were swirling in the beams from the lights.

" I wonder why they are doing this? Hell, they'll have to exterminate all the gulls on the coast if it keeps up."

" David, I don't want to talk about it anymore tonight. Please," she begged.

As he turned the car into the hotel parking lot and entered the ramp, Marina felt calmer. Just being off the street and away from the night sky made her feel better. The tires squealed as David went from one level to the next looking for a parking space. Finally, he found a spot. As he pulled the car up against the retaining wall, he could see the gulls in the distance flying over the hotel at the end of the boardwalk.

GULLS

Marina didn't notice them and David wasn't about to point them out to her. Once inside the elevator, she finally felt safe.

Exiting the elevator on the main floor put them into a lobby filled with people. The casino was acres of slot machines, gambling tables and thousands of people. David soon saw the marquee for the concert and he took Marina's hand and led her through the crowd to the corridor leading to the concert.

The air conditioning felt good as they made their way into the hall. The usher walked with them to their aisle and they were quick to sit down. The concert had been sold out and they were close to being late for the show. The free tickets were good seats for the concert. In front of them was a circular stage that was turning slowly. Overhead, David watched as four men maneuvered booms out over the audience. A bank of lights encircled the stage and was positioned about thirty feet overhead. Shortly, white smoke appeared from under the stage. Someone switched on some light blue lights and the smoke now crept along the floor and reflected a beautiful, heavenly looking atmosphere.

The band was split into groups in the inside of the circular stage. Six vocalists that were backup singers for the performer arranged their microphones. Suddenly, a synthesizer being played by the lead keyboard player came alive. His right hand was positioned over the upper octave keys on the keyboard and he continued a rapid fingering of the high notes. Without warning, his left hand plunged onto the keyboard and electrifying bass notes filled the room with sound.

Everyone looked in the direction of the stage door for the performer. Suddenly, laser beams of lights flashed in succession over the audience. They were timed with the beat of the music as the keyboard was joined by the drummer and an erotic and rhythmic beat filled the room. Still, the performer did not appear. A cylinder of white mesh material dropped from the ceiling and the laser beams were focused on it. As the stage moved in a circle in one direction, the white cylinder in the center of the stage, moved in the opposite direction. Quickly, through the innovation of special effects, the white cylinder began to change color and the music grew louder. Now the audience was sure that the cylinder would be raised and the performer would appear in the center of it all. The vocalists began harmonizing and the synthesizer continued to add more volumes of music. Then, the volume decreased. The voices from the six singers harmonized perfectly as the performer's voice was heard from within the cylinder.

" Lonely looking sky, lonely sky, lonely looking sky," he sang.

The audience broke into a tremendous applause as Neil Diamond began his song. His band continued to add the necessary harmonizing as he continued singing. Suddenly, the cylinder began to lift and the performer stood in the center. Somehow, a recording of ocean waves was added to the sound of the synthesizer and to his voice.

" Sleep, we sleep ... for we may dream, while we may dream" he continued to sing.

His concert opened with the ballad, " Jonathan Livingston Seagull."

Marina and David sat watching as the cylinder lifted and Neil Diamond stood not more than fifty feet in front of them. As the volume of the music increased and the lights focused on him, a flock of gulls was released from under the stage. They took off in all directions and circled over the audience. Marina's scream could be heard over the band and the vocalist. Ushers started running down the aisles, thinking that something serious had taken place. David could not stop Marina from screaming.

All at once, the music stopped and Neil Diamond stood waiting for the commotion to end. With the help of the ushers, Marina was escorted from the auditorium. They were taken to a room in the hotel and the hotel doctor was called immediately.

" Please. Take me home, David,"she pleaded through her uncontrollable sobbing as the doctor checked her over.

" It'll be all right, we'll go back to the beach house right now,"he assured her.

Marina and David returned home to the Rutledge Place, and to Chris and Kathleen. The concert was more than Marina could deal with. The vacation that had turned into her worst nightmare. Before going to sleep, she made David promise that as soon as Erica was released from the hospital, they would return immediately to Kansas.

CHAPTER TEN:

The Posse

They gathered, as usual, at the arcade located at the north end of the island.

" I say we shoot the damned things."

Standing in the center of the group was Barry Davis. This was his twelfth summer on the island. Immediately after graduation from high school, his mother packed for the annual summer vacation. While she spent every night in front of the television, Barry visited the arcade and met with his friends. With him was his girlfriend Amy Bensen. She looked like the stereotypical California blonde, transplanted to New Jersey. Five feet two inches tall and the most brilliant golden hair. Barry was still trying to impress Amy, even though she tried to convince him that they would be together till the end of time, he felt the need to continually show off for her.

" Barry, don't be crazy. You can't kill every gull on the island," Amy told him.

" Yea, well we can put a helluva dent in the flock and have a good time doing it."

" I'm in with you," added Brad, Barry's best friend on the island.

Brad was playing one of the video games half listening to Barry.

The decision had been made. Inside of an hour they all met back in the parking lot. They were now armed with rifles and pistols. Nine four-wheel-drive vehicles of all types were loaded with the teenagers and the hunt was about to begin.

They moved their assortment of Jeeps and buggies onto the beach. All of them had high powered lights mounted on the roll bars or roofs. One by one, they switched on the lights and aimed the vehicles to the north beaches. There was no one in front of them. Only the night sea mist that had moved in blocked their vision of the sandy runway that lay in front of them. The lights peered through the mist.

" Can't see a fuckin' thing out here," one of them yelled out.

He was quickly drowned out by the sound of their engines revving up. They waited for Barry to give the signal.

" Hey ! Catch," Barry called to Brad.

The headlight of the Jeep behind him caught the silver from the can of cold beer that he had thrown from his Bronco over to Brad's old Jeep Renegade.

" Throw me another one," Brad demanded.

Immediately, Barry threw another can. Before it could reach him, Barry released the clutch of his

Bronco and the four-wheel drive leapt forward. The girls sat in the back of the vehicles and the boys stood leaning against the roll bars or the windshield with a can or bottle of beer in one hand, and a weapon in the other. The posse began the high speed search along the beach.

" Over there !" Someone yelled from the speeding chariot.

Without warning, the first shot from a shotgun was fired in the direction of the sand dunes, followed by the second shot that was fired toward the breakers. The explosion of the twelve gauge shells was followed by the yelling from all of them as the race along the beach continued.

Barry looked down at the speedometer and noticed that they were going fifty miles an hour. Brad soon came alongside of him and looked over at Barry. Letting out a yell like an indian brave on a war path, Brad yelled and then took another gulp of beer. Barry pushed the pedal closer to the floor board of the Bronco and it pulled away from Brad's Jeep.

" There !" someone else screamed, and a series of shots were fired into the night air. Suddenly, without warning, Barry down shifted the Bronco and turned the steering wheel toward the dunes. As he drove the vehicle into the soft sand, he could feel the sloppy and sluggish steering take over. Still, he applied even more gas to the engine and glanced into the mirror to watch the pack following his lead.

" Over there !" Amy yelled out, pointing at the sand dunes.

GULLS

An albatross heard the oncoming posse and took to the air. The almost ten-pound bird just became airborne when one of Brad's companions aimed the rifle and fired. The bird fell to the sand like a rock being thrown.

" All right !" Brad screamed out.

The bird flew high enough that the headlights reflected the underside of its wings. It became an easy target for them. Soon, they decided to split up, and the group of hunters spread out over the beach. Shots were being fired in all directions and for the next fifteen minutes, the sound of rifles and of engines scared up even more gulls.

" Look, over there," Amy called out.

" All right ! " Barry, headed in the direction of a group of gulls that were perched on the top of a sand dune. He downshifted the Bronco again and aimed it in the direction of the flock. Looking over his shoulder to the left, he could see another Bronco headed in the same direction. Although he couldn't see exactly who was driving or exactly which Bronco it was, he could see the teenaged marksman aiming his rifle in the direction of the flock of birds.

" Faster," Amy called.

The Bronco started sliding to the right as they approached the dunes.

" Hang on !" Barry screamed, as the Bronco started up the sand dune and the gulls took to the air in front of him. He knew that directly on the other side of the row of sand dunes, were the thick bayberry bushes. Unable to stop the Bronco, or to turn it away from the top of the dunes, Barry lost control. The front of the Bronco slammed into the soft sand and the rear of the vehicle bucked up and over. Amy was thrown from the Bronco and landed in the soft sand a few yards away. The cooler of beer flew from the back seat and was hurled out into the bushes. The Bronco came to a stop, upside down, in the thick bayberry bushes. For a short time, the engine remained running. Soon, it stopped and Barry could hear the steam from the radiator as the water escaped from a gaping hole and sprayed onto the hot engine. The white steam mixed with the mist and enveloped the Bronco in a close canopy of condensation.

" Fuck !" Barry called out. " Amy, where are you?" he called in a panic.

" Over here,"she yelled out to him.

" God damn it," he said to himself in almost a whisper. " You okay?" he asked.

" I think so," she answered. "Yea, I'm okay."

Barry crawled the rest of the way from under the Bronco and stood beside it looking in the direction of Amy's voice.

" Real smart, Barry,"

He didn't answer. He was more glad that Amy was not hurt than anything else. The headlights of the Bronco were buried into the sand. The lights on the roll bars were now just a foot off the sand and they gave Barry a good look at the steam that was billowing from under the hood.

Amy soon joined him, standing beside the upturned Bronco. They were soon distracted from appraising the situation. The sound of sirens could be heard approaching the north beach.

" Oh, shit."

" Get down," he instructed Amy.

Barry quickly crawled under the Bronco and turned the knob that would kill the lights on the Bronco. He was sure that, if caught, they would be in serious trouble. Barry figured that they could just leave the Bronco in the sand dunes for the night, and right side the vehicle in the morning.

Storming down the beach was a group of Brigantine Island Police. Barry crawled to the top of the sand dune and along with Amy, they watched as the vehicles went speeding past them. Within seconds, they had stopped the first of the gull hunters. Barry could see the Jeep stopped on the hard sand and the headlights from two police cars shining on the apprehended group. The night mist made it difficult for them to see which one of their friend's were being questioned by the police.

They heard the sound of a speeding Chevy Blazer, moving in their direction, with no lights on at all. It passed them and continued down the beach, escaping the police. Barry knew that whoever it was would dodge the searching police.

" We'll wait here," Barry said.

" All night?" Amy asked.

" No. Just 'til they're gone, then we can walk back. Mom's going to shit if she finds out about this."

Barry had a knack for talking his way out of most things. Since his father died, he could get away with most anything, and he took full advantage of it. In a way, he was the envy of most of his friends because he could do anything that he wanted. As long as his grades in school were good, he was more or less on his own. But this, he felt, would be enough to get him into major trouble.

" Leave the beach," the voice said through the loud-speaker.

The police decided that it would be easier to instruct whomever was out on the beach to simply leave the beach.

" This beach is closed," the voice continued. " Leave it now, return to the island immediately."

" Should we go now?" Amy asked Barry.

" No. We'll wait it out. They'll leave soon and then we can go."

Just after the announcement, a set of headlights came on in a Jeep parked against the sand dunes. It began moving slowly down the beach. The police watched as it made its way to the residential half of the island. They had hoped that they would be heard by everyone out on the beach and that this would put an end to the mayhem. Soon, they drove their police cars along the beach at the edge of the water and repeated the message over and over.

When all was quiet again, Barry and Amy walked along the sand, laughing about the entire episode. In the morning they would return with Brad and retrieve the Bronco from the dunes. They did consider themselves lucky that they were not hurt. They were sure that they would be the topic of conversation at the arcade for the remainder of the summer. Barry knew that, eventually, his mother would find out about the incident, but he promised himself that he would deal with it then instead of now.

CHAPTER ELEVEN:
Evening Magazine

The satellite link between the BBC, in London, England and the International Broadcasting Network, IBS, New York, had been quickly arranged. Also, the affiliate stations from Los Angeles and Florida were standing by for the cue. In New York, the evening magazine show was preparing to go live with a full one hour report on the gull attacks. On the floor in the New York networks studio "A" was the evening news anchor, Margaret Hunt. The floor director went through his usual routine of yelling orders to the floor staff.

" Stand by people ! We have two minutes till air," he yelled.

In the director's booth, the overhead monitors displayed the many camera views of all the sets. In England, the host was positioned between two guests. In Florida, the guest sat on the stage alone, waiting for the cue. And, in Los Angeles, the stage had four chairs, in each was seated an expert on wildfowl and seabirds. Preparation for this special had been hasty.

GULLS

Within three days, the network pulled together this assortment of experts. The decision was to try to get a jump on the other networks and the print media by staging this special one hour broadcast.

" We're on in fifty," the floor director announced.

In the booth in New York, the director watched the large red numerals as they revealed the seconds counting down to air time.

" Stand by on the floor. Stand by LA. Stand by Florida," he called through his pin microphone that he was wearing.

" Standby to roll tape."

The TV monitor in front of him was a scrambled picture of something. Suddenly, it stopped. On monitor number one in all the studios was a picture of a tern. The black head and wing tips, were a familiar sight to everyone. The bird was the most recognized of the sea gull species.

" Standby, music."

The sound man was turning two reels of audio tape with his index finger tip of both hands. Satisfied that he had arrived at the precise position on the tape, he sat waiting for the cue.

" In, five, four, three."

" Roll tape," the director exclaimed.

The picture of the sea gull began moving in slow motion. The music was a full orchestra score that had been recorded for this special. As the strings harmonized with the sound of ocean waves, the title "Gulls" appeared on the TV screen.

Margaret Hunt sat in the center of the stage. Behind

her was a projected image of the same thing that was being seen by the television audience. Soon, the director would dissolve the image to that of the anchor, Margaret Hunt, with the continuation of the film footage being projected in the background. As soon as the titles were finished, he cued the floor to standby.

The floor director held out his left hand with four fingers opened wide. simultaneous with the count from the director in the booth, he flashed his hand beside the camera, signaling the countdown, four, three, two, one.

" Good evening. Welcome to tonight's special edition of Newsfront," Margret Hunt said. "In light of this weeks strange news item that has been coming in from around the world, involving the sporadic attack of sea gulls on some of the most popular beach resorts, we at Newsfront decided to devote the entire hour to sea gulls, their behavior, their origan, and their lifestyle."

Margaret Hunt had been the evening network news anchor for the last three years. She began her career at an affiliate station in Philadelphia. Her relaxed style was soon recognized by the network and Margaret found herself in the "Big Leagues". Her short, five feet tall slender body presented some unique problems for the director. Care had to be given to camera angles that would not make her appear too short or too small to the audience. Margaret was seasoned as a news anchor and could read the teleprompter with ease. Her jet black hair set off her copper colored eyes and she looked very good on camera. Her attractiveness combined with a natural smile conveyed to the audience that she was a comfortable host. For this broadcast, she had been rehearsed so the entire one hour special would go off without a hitch.

" Before we talk with some experts about the aggressiveness and attitude of the gulls. We would like you to understand their behavior. For that, we have consulted the National Geographic Society and have obtained this footage from a recent episode of "Salt Water Birds."

" Standby on tape," the director called out to the people in the booth.

" Roll tape, in three, two," he continued.

The camera backed away from Margaret and the television screens flipped to the footage from the Geographic special. For the next thirty-five minutes, the audience saw an informative and fascinating biography on sea gulls and their behavior. Suddenly, sea gulls became the focus of all the news media not only on IBS but every TV network and tabloid.

*

Byron drove along the beach in his Jeep looking for gulls. He was nearing the extreme end of the island, where the bay met with the ocean. That was where the stock pile of clam shells had been placed by the excavating crew. He could see the driver of the bulldozer seated in the mammoth piece of equipment puffing on a cigarette. His legs were stretched out in front of him and his feet were placed on the protective screen. On his lap, he had a thirty eight caliber pistol, loaded and ready if needed. The gulls swooped and circled directly overhead, waiting for him to start the engine and bulldoze a fresh supply of clam shells from under the mountain. The air was saturated with the odor of decaying clams. Byron tried not to let the smell bother him as he got even closer to the machine. He wondered why the odor didn't seem to bother the driver. He thought to himself that there would be no way that he could do that job. The dozer driver noticed Byron's Jeep approaching and jumped down from the yellow metallic man made mastodon as Byron was nearing. He didn't leave the safety of the protective cage of the dozer without taking the pistol.

Suddenly, he turned to the mountain of shells and fired the pistol in its direction. Byron couldn't see from his vantage point, but he was sure that the man had shot one of the gulls and that it had fallen onto the mountain of shells. He fired the gun again, this time almost directly over his head. This time a gull fell from the sky and landed near his feet. He kicked it aside. After sticking the gun barrel into his belt, he continued walking toward Byron.

"Wanna' shot?" he called out.

"Whaddaya know?" Byron called out, ignoring the question the man had asked as his Jeep rolled to a stop.

"It's hot and smelly,"the worker answered watching

the gulls circle the mountain of shells.

" How are the gulls?"

" Fuck. They're disgusting. God damned rats, all they do is eat and shit. Half the time they shit on me."

Byron noticed that the dark blue coveralls that the man was wearing had white and yellow spatters all over them. Until the man mentioned the gulls' behavior, he thought they were old paint spots. In fact, the guy was spattered with gull droppings.

" If I shot every gull that took a shit on me today, there wouldn't be a gull left on the island."

" Have any of them come after you?" Byron asked.

" No. Nothin'' like that. They're too fuckin' busy eating and fighting with each other. Let me tell ya, I never realized what filthy animals these things are till I took this job."

Behind the man, the gulls flew and fought with each other

over the mountain of clam shells. The noise from their screaming at each other was incredible.

" Those big bastards over there. They're the worst," he said as he pointed to the albatross.

The large dirty brown colored birds could weigh as much as eight pounds. For the most part, they kept to themselves. At times, however, they would swoop in on the other birds and steal whatever morsels the terns had uncovered.

For now, the attempt at keeping the gulls away from the populated beaches was working. As Byron carried on idle conversation with the man, he watched the gulls and their behavior. He didn't see anything out of the ordinary. Occasionally, the ocean breeze would bring some relief to the stench in the air. The salt water breeze was a refreshing change. But when it stopped, the hot humid and stinking smell would close in on him.

" Well, see ya. Wouldn't want to be ya," Byron said.

" Hey, it's a job," the man replied.

As Byron turned to get back into the Jeep, he noticed a few more gulls coming in from out at sea. They never paid any attention to him or the man. Instead, they joined the rest of the carnivorous scavengers at the pile of decomposing seafood. Byron came to see what was going on with the gulls, but couldn't wait to get the hell out of there. He swore to himself that he would never be back either.

As he started the Jeep, he began turning the steering wheel so as to not waste any time getting out of the area. Anything he could do to hurry himself out of there would be good. He felt the bottom of his stomach rise to somewhere just below his Adam's apple. It was all he could do to keep from heaving. Fortunately, he was able to escape to fresher air as he sped along the hardened sand in the direction of the Rutledge Place, six miles away at the other end of the island.

Byron had been studying the behavior of all types of birds, including sea birds for almost all of his life. This, he thought, was without a doubt the most bizarre thing that he had ever heard of. There must be a reason for the attacks. Why wasn't the man with the dozer attacked by any of the hundreds of gulls that were circling him? Could it be the availability of food.

That is what everyone had speculated. Byron, had a gut feeling, though, that there was another reason for the attacks. He was determined to find out what it was. As he continued along the beach, he put together some questions in his mind that he would ask the Spencer family when he got to the Rutledge Place. In the meantime, he slowed the Jeep as he approached the populated beaches on the south half of the island.

CHAPTER TWELVE:

Do Not Feed Them

At the Rutledge Place, Marina remained in the upper bedroom. The curtains were open and the afternoon sun stayed focused, uninterrupted by passing clouds on the beaches and water. She could see that people were sunbathing and walking the beach with total disregard of that fact that the gulls were still out there somewhere. She sat in the easy chair trying to read a magazine that David had bought for her. Chris was busy watching an afternoon movie. David had gone back to the computer conference in Atlantic City and Kathleen had gone shopping in town. It was difficult for Marina to focus on the stories in the magazine. Instead, she just flipped through the pages, looking at the photographs of featured celebrities.

Outside the Rutledge Place, just on the other side of a few sand dunes, was a small cottage. Marina had noticed that it appeared empty. Since they had been there, she saw no one around the place. Now, she noticed that there were some clothes hanging on a clothes line beside the house. The white sheets flapped in the ocean breeze like surrender flags as a signal to someone at sea.

GULLS

In a few minutes an old woman appeared. Marina had thought that she was returning to remove the clothes from the line. Instead, she had a cooking pot under her left arm. Still caught up in a pictorial about Julia Roberts in the magazine, Marina half paid attention to the old woman. Suddenly, the woman began throwing something into the air.

" My God !" Marina said as she threw the magazine aside. "She'll entice all the gulls to her."

The woman continued to throw the scraps to the air. At first nothing happened. The woman looked up at the sky and then looked around to the sand dunes. She was curious as to why there were no gulls. Each afternoon she had done the same thing over and over, year after year. Always the gulls would come to take away the scraps of food that she would present to them. Again, she threw the food to the air but it fell to the sand unnoticed. From Marina's vantage point in the room on the third level of the house, she could see the first of the gulls as it traveled along the beach. She knew that if one would come, they all would come.

The woman continued her search for the gulls. She waited some time before throwing any more of the food into the air. Marina realized what would take place. Feeling that she had little time, and that the woman had obviously not heard about
the gull attacks, Marina stood from her chair. She was feeling a combination of fear and desperation - desperate to stop the woman from continuing the feeding and fear that she would be attacked herself. But she couldn't let it continue. The second and third gull

appeared over the beach. Then, Marina noticed other gulls coming from over the rooftops from the west. That was it. She knew that she would have to get to the old woman before the gulls did.

" No. Stop it !" she yelled into the emptiness of the room.

She started her run for the stairs and for the door on the first level. As she darted across the bedroom in the direction of the stairs, she stumbled. Knocking the side table with her hip, she managed to upset a vase from the table surface. Thinking she could stop the vase from falling, she tried desperately to grab the cut glass relic but failed. As it tumbled onto the glass top table it broke. Unfortunately, it had broken just before Marina reached for it. A sliver of glass slit her arm just above the wrist and she bled profusely. She had no time to stop and deal with the cut. Running down the stairs she grabbed at her wrist. In front of her she could see the woman through the windows, she was still throwing food for the gulls.

" Damn it! Stop!" Marina yelled.

The gulls drew closer to the house. By the time that Marina had reached the front door, the gulls had arrived over the cottage. The front door deadbolt had been locked and Marina tried desperately to unlock it. The blood from her gash in her arm flew against the wooden surface of the door and her hand slid on the warm wet surface as she fumbled with the locked knob.

" Damn it come on," she yelled to herself.

Outside, the gulls gathered. It seemed that they

GULLS

came from out of nowhere. By the time Marina had opened the door, there were dozens of them. Now, she couldn't see the cottage or the woman feeding the gulls. The sand dunes blocked her vision. But she knew that she would have to hurry to get to the woman in time. As soon as she saw the soft sand stretched in front of her, she remembered the attack on Erica. For a split second, she hesitated just outside the door. The afternoon heat hit her in the face and the smell of the ocean filled her nostrils. Over the sand dunes, the woman stood with her kitchen pot. They gathered around her, hovering, looking for more food. Without any more hesitation, Marina began running through the sand and onto the sand dune. At first she slipped and fell into the sand. Picking herself up, she began the struggle again.

Emotions ran through her as she climbed the sand, trying to get her legs to help her up the hill of sand faster. She squeezed her wrist more tightly as she felt the increasing pain from the cut. She remembered the image of Erica lying in the sand with the gulls on top of her. Please, she thought, don't let this be another episode of terror. Reaching the top of the dune, she saw the gulls. Again, by the hundreds, they encircled the expectant victim.

From the other side of the dunes, Byron approached in his Jeep. Unsuspecting of what he was about to see, he turned the Jeep in the direction of the Rutledge Place and left the hard surface of the wet sand onto the hot soft sand that led to the contemporary house. He saw the gulls circling over the dunes.

" Stop," Marina yelled out to the old woman.

Paying no regard to the calls from Marina, the woman continued to throw the last of the scraps of food to the air. As Marina ran down the sand dune she fell. Picking herself up from the hot granules she tried not to think of what she would soon be seeing. The gulls screamed in excitement as they swirled around the woman.

" Stop !"

Much to Marina's surprise, the woman was still on her feet. Having just finished throwing the last of the morsels to the air, she was turning to go back to her house as she saw Marina running from the sand dune. Marina was still screaming for the woman to stop. Most of the birds had finished the feeding and had turned and flew out to sea again. Some had remained and were perched on the sand whining for some additional food. But, there were no attacks on either Marina or the old woman.

" What's wrong, my dear?" the woman asked.

" Aren't you afraid of being attacked by them?"

" Why, no, don't be silly. I have been feeding the gulls for years. Why should I be afraid?"

" Haven't you heard the news? Haven't you heard about the gulls attacking?"

" Don't be silly. Gulls won't hurt you."

Marina was surprised that the woman didn't hear about the gull attacks.

" What happened to your arm?" the woman asked.

" I'll be all right,"Marina said as she held her bleeding wrist.

GULLS

Just then, Marina heard Byron's Jeep approach the house from the other side of the sand dunes.

" I just wanted to be sure that you were all right. I thought they would attack you. I'm sorry, I didn't mean to scare you."

" Why don't you come in? Let me look at your arm. It looks like a bad cut."

" No. that's all right. I'll clean it up at home."

Marina couldn't help looking at the sky for gulls while she was talking with the woman. She really just wanted to get off the beach and get back inside where she would feel safe. A few gulls stood in the sand watching as she talked with the old woman. Marina didn't take her eyes off of them.

" I have to be going. I'll be okay," she assured the woman.

When she reached the front door of the Rutledge Place she found Byron at the front door that was standing open.

" Can I help you?" she said as she approached the house.

" Mrs. Spencer, I was just wondering if I could ask you some questions."

Just then he noticed that she was hurt. Marina was still holding her wrist and the blood that she had lost a few minutes earlier was streaking her arm.

" Looks like you've been hurt. Here, let me look at that," he asked.

" I think I'll be fine," she responded as she removed her hand from her right wrist. It was apparent that she had a deep cut and that it would require some stitches. Byron offered to take her to the hospital to get some stitches and to see a Doctor. He felt that this would be a good opportunity to ask Marina some questions regarding Erica.

While they drove down Brigantine Blvd. leaving the island for Atlantic City and the hospital, Byron questioned Marina about the attack on Erica by the gulls.

" Is there anything you can remember that would lead you to think that the gulls would attack Erica?"

" No, nothing. She just wanted to feed them the popcorn. It all seemed normal. They came from all over. I didn't really see anything at first, except the gulls flying and hovering over her head."

Byron continued asking Marina all sorts of questions but there was nothing unusual about the whole thing. Byron had watched hundreds of kids feed the gulls. By the time they reached the hospital, Byron had learned nothing unusual about the incident that would lead him to believe of a reason for the attack.

❋

The cameras were focused on Margaret Hunt who sat waiting again for the cue from the floor director and for the red light on the top of the camera to light that would signal her to look into it.

" In our studio in Los Angeles is perhaps the foremost expert on sea birds and by far the most informed on sea gulls," she began. " Dwight Taylor is a professor of wildlife at California's Institute of Wildlife and has recently finished an in depth study of sea gulls for the most accurate recording of the birds and their habitat," she continued as she turned and faced Dwight Taylor.

" Mister Taylor, we understand that you have input into your computers, all the available information concerning the gull attacks?"

" Yes, Margaret, we have."

" Are their any coincidences between the gull attack of Erica Spencer in New Jersey and the attacks that took place in Europe?"

" No. Not as far as we can tell. We have input all the information that is available to us. The types of gulls that they were; the time of day of each attack; the weather conditions and the typographical information. There doesn't seem to be any correlation between the events or the people."

Dwight squinted his eyes from the bright lights that were being used. His white hair and beard added to his credibility on camera.

" I have traveled all over the world in my studies of sea birds. Never have I known this type of behavior from sea gulls. I can only speculate that it has something to do with the feeding habits. All of the attacks occurred on moderately populated beaches, where it is common for people to be feeding the birds. Once the supply was stopped, it may have caused them to be all the more aggressive."

" Yes, Mr Taylor, we have heard that speculation," Margaret continued. " There doesn't seem to be a connection though with the people on the beaches where the attacks occurred. For instance, Leslie, the girl from Brigantine Island, who was killed by the gulls. She apparently was picked out from hundreds of people on the beach. As a matter of fact, the investigation revealed that Leslie had been sunbathing on a deserted part of the island and the birds found her and preyed on her as though she were the enemy."

" There doesn't seem to be a clear answer for these attacks," Dwight continued. " In the case of the six people on the beaches of the Mediterranean Sea, they were selected out of a crowded beach of hundreds of people. There doesn't seem to be a connection between them. We have, however, noticed that the attacks only occur where people are swimming. There are, as you may know, gulls in the parking lots of shopping centers, well inland. There have not been any reported attacks from people there. Also, there are gulls hanging around dumps and, for instance, even trailing behind ocean vessels. There have not been any reported attacks there either."

" Standby Florida," the director called out so that he could be heard over everyone's earphones.

" We also have with us, a panel of experts on wildlife. Our affiliate station WFLA TV, Miami, Florida, has been standing by with the panel who has been studying the situation of the gull attacks since they began last week."

The picture on the television screen split and showed Dwight Taylor on one half and the anchor from the Florida affiliate on the other half.

GULLS

" Good evening, Mister. O'Grady," Margaret stated.

" Good evening, Margaret, and good evening Mister. Taylor."

" Mister. O'Grady, you have been listening to Dwight Taylor. Do you have any information that could shed some light on the subject?" Margaret continued.

"Well, I hate to say this," Mister. O'Grady said. " But, I guess you could call all of us gullible. No pun intended. But, these attacks have all taken place on the beaches of the middle or the upper class. I know I'll hear a lot about this. But, we have shared the information with our colleague from California and our computer has been able to tell us that none of the attacks have taken place on our public beaches where the lower class normally congregate. All of the attacks have taken place on the beaches usually visited by the middle or even the upper class."

" You can't be saying that the gulls are passing up poor people for the wealthy, are you?" Margaret quizzed. " I think that the audience would think you're crazy for saying that ."

" That they may," he continued. " The fact is this. I mean so far, none of the gull attacks have taken place on any other beaches. It may sound silly, but the computer has only come up with that comparison."

" Are you saying that it may be too early to tell anything? Does the computer have enough information in order to come up with anything? A possible answer."

" Please realize that this is all new to all of us. The

investigations into the attacks haven't revealed anything at this time. We can't expect the computer to give us the answer to solve the mystery.

" How about lotions?" Margaret asked. " Someone had pointed out that they could be attracted to the smell of cocoa oil or some of the newer sunscreens that had been used at the beach and elsewhere."

"Well, we took that into consideration. Yes, all of the people that were attacked had been using lotions. But suntan lotions are used by most everyone at the beach. There doesn't seem to be any connection to the lotions. If so, the attacks would most certainly occur over a more widespread area and also there would be more attacks."

The broadcast continued with no answer to the problem. Margaret conducted the interviews having never reached a clear answer to the mystery.

" Authorities continue to caution, that until they find out exactly why the gulls are attacking, we should be very careful on the beaches where gulls tend to congregate. We certainly hope that this broadcast gave you more insight into the behavior of these most picturesque and romantic birds. We also want to warn you that there doesn't appear to be anywhere that is absolutely safe from the sudden attack by them. Should you be attacked by these birds of prey, we would like you to call the toll free number being shown on your screen. Any information could help in searching for the reason for the attacks and will help to make our beaches safe again."

Margaret looked down at the teleprompter that was

positioned in the top of the desk in front of her and then looked up.

" This sad but tragic news has just been reported. Tonya Neil, identical twin sister of Leslie Neil, had been in Atlantic City, New Jersey, as Michigan's contestant for this year's Miss America Pageant. Her sister Leslie was the first fatality from the gull attacks. She was killed on Brigantine Island, New Jersey. Tonya has withdrawn from the Miss America Pageant and will be returning to Michigan with her parents. Linda Meddula will be taking Tonya's place as the contestant from the state of Michigan. For Newsfront, I'm Margaret Hunt, Good night."

" We're clear," the director announced.

✳

CHAPTER THIRTEEN:
Let's Get Out of Here

David and Marina made the daily visit to the hospital and had just returned home to the Rutledge Place when the phone rang.

" Rutledge Place," Kathleen answered.

" This is Doctor White. Is Mister or Mrs. Spencer there?"

" Why yes, Doctor, they are. I'll be callin' the Mrs to the phone in just a minute. Would ya' hold please."

Marina and David had gone into the den to see Chris when Kathleen called into the room.

" This is Mrs. Spencer. Hello."

" This is Dr. White. I'm sorry I missed you. The nurses tell me that I just arrived shortly after you had gone. It's about Erica.

I have examined her, and I think that we can go ahead and release her tomorrow. I do still want to see her for a few days. I thought I had better talk with you first. I know you are wanting to return to Kansas, but I would really like to see Erica in a couple of days. Then you can go ahead back to Kansas."

" Wonderful, Doctor. Thank you so much for calling. I guess we can stay here for a few more days. When can we get Erica? When can we bring her home?"

" You can take her home tomorrow. The hospital likes to have the patients that are leaving check out before noon."

" That'll be fine, I'm sure," Marina said.

" Okay I'll go ahead and tell Erica that she can go home tomorrow. Oh, and please try to keep her calm. I mean, she will continue to need rest. I'll talk more about that when I see you at the office."

" Thank you, Doctor."

" Goodbye, Marina."

David was standing directly behind Marina, trying to establish the nature of the conversation by the way that Marina was talking.

" Erica can come home tomorrow," Marina told him as she buried her face into his shoulder.

" Super. I'll have to go in to the convention in the morning, just for a few last minute things, then I can come home and take you to get Erica."

" Okay. But Doctor White said that we can't leave for Kansas until he sees Erica for the next couple of days. You know how much I want to get out of here."

" Yes. But I think a few more days will be all right."

Chris couldn't take it much longer. He had been cooped up in the house for nearly a week and played every video game at least a hundred times. Kathleen had her hands full trying to keep him busy while Marina was at the hospital and while David was at the convention in Atlantic City. So when the call came in from Byron, Chris was more than happy. Byron wanted to take Chris with him on his rounds of the island.

" Mrs. Spencer, I promise you that Chris will be all right," Byron told her.

" But, what about the gulls?"

" There hasn't been an attack by the gulls in the last three days. Besides, there aren't any gulls on this part of that island. It's safe, believe me."

" I don't know, Byron. His father may object. Let me talk it over with him and I'll call you back."

Byron planned to spend the day with Christopher. They planned to check on all the nests that Byron had been documenting and they would tour the entire north end of the island. Byron thought this would give him an opportunity to get closer to the Spencer's and maybe find out something more about the gull attack on Erica. He was sure that he would be able to discover the reason for the attacks, if he asked enough questions.

Marina talked it over with David and, finally, they decided that as long as Byron kept him away from the gulls, it would be okay.

Erica would be home tomorrow, so Marina spent most of the evening getting things ready for her. Occasionally, there was a knock at the front door and Kathleen would send the news people away. They were still trying to interview the family, but Marina would not have it.

Byron arrived at the Rutledge Place early. The

GULLS

Spencer's had just finished breakfast and were sitting around the table talking about how nice it would be to have Erica home again.

" I'll just be happy to get off the island and get back to Kansas," Marina told them.

" I'm afraid this just wasn't a very good vacation for ya, was it, Ma'am?"

" No, Kathleen, it wasn't. I don't care if I ever see the beach again...or another sea gull."

" If it wasn't for Doctor White wanting to see Erica in a couple of days, I would leave this morning."

" When will ya' be gettin' her, ma'am?"

" David and I will go shortly and we'll be back early this afternoon."

" And the boy, when will he be back?"

Just then, Byron rang the bell and Christopher ran to answer the door.

" Good mornin', Chris," Byron said.

" Morning, sir."

" Just call me Byron, David. Calling me sir just makes me feel old."

" Okay, Byron. We leavin' now?"

" In a minute. Where's your mom and dad?"

" In the kitchen. C'mon !"Chris said as he ran down the hall toward the kitchen.

The excitement of getting out of the house and spending the day with Byron made Chris more than a little happy. Marina was on her way down the long hall to meet Byron when she saw that they were heading for the kitchen.

" Would you like some coffee?" Marina offered.

" No, thanks. I just finished a cup."

" You'll be careful, won't you Byron? Don't let him near the gulls."

" Yes, ma'am. Chris'll be fine." If you want to talk to Chris while I'm out there, here's the number.

Byron handed Marina his calling card. In the upper corner was an official looking seal with an eagle foil stamped in the center of something that ended with "... of the United States." Under the name Byron Jackson were the words " Research Specialist."

The dispatcher could connect Byron with Marina on a special cellular phone line.

" We're bringing Erica home from the hospital this afternoon. I would like Chris to be here. He hasn't seen her since the attack."

" Well, just call when you get back and we can be here ina few minutes."

" That'll be fine," David added.

" Chris, be sure you listen to everything Byron tells you to do," Marina instructed. " Stay close to Byron and behave yourself."

" He'll be fine. We'll have a good time,"Byron guaranteed her.

After Marina kissed Christopher, Chris and Byron left immediately. Chris sat in the Jeep scanning over all the radios. In the rear seat, Byron had the red cooler that was filled with ice and had plenty of cold drinks. After a little trouble starting the engine, Byron turned the steering wheel and headed for the beach. Already, some people were out on the sand. They could see some beach umbrellas scattered on the beach. The morning air was clear. The sun had not yet distorted the air over the sand and they could see clearly as Byron sped along the wet sand. Chris liked the way that the water flew off the tires and occasionally blew into the Jeep. The cold water felt good. Byron pushed the gas pedal harder and the Jeep cruised along the sand with little effort.

When they reached the end of the beaches where people could swim, Chris noticed that there were no lifeguard stands along the rest of the beaches.

" This is where the bird sanctuary begins," Byron told him.

" Dad said you can't swim down here."

" That's right. There aren't any lifeguards. It wouldn't be safe."

Just then, he turned the steering wheel and headed for the soft sand and toward the sand dunes. They approached the part of the island where Leslie was attacked. This time, there were no gulls to be found.

" I don't see any sea gulls," Chris yelled out over the sound of the roaring engine.

" They're all out at the end of the island. There aren't any around here now. We'll stay clear of them."

Byron slowed the Jeep as he climbed the first sand dune. Chris lifted himself slightly from the seat to try to see over the top of the dune before the Jeep reached it. On the other side, Chris could see the smaller dunes that were rising from the bushes. Byron slowed the vehicle even more as he worked it through the bushes. Some of the branches brushed the sides of the Jeep and soon they found themselves driving through a maze of bayberry bushes and tall grass. To Chris, it was like taking an exploration through the jungle.

Byron stopped and took a hand-drawn map from between the seats.

" You lost?" Chris asked.

" No. We have a lot of nests to look at this morning. Once we find the first one, we'll be able to follow our tire tracks to the rest. Unless the wind has blown the tracks away. I just have to find the first one. This is my map, ya see."

Chris looked at the map with Byron. It was all meaningless to him but he felt that he wanted to be a part of the exploration.

" Here. Over here," Byron said as he glanced out to the left of the Jeep.

He stuffed the map down between the seats again, and they headed back into the tall bushes. Suddenly, Chris could see the tire tracks made in the white sand from the Jeep's many trips to the same area. The branches rubbed and scratched along the sides of the Jeep and occasionally, they would make a sound similar to nails on a blackboard. All of a sudden, Byron pushed the pedal down more and they went faster along his man made road in the sand.

" Here. Here we are," he said as he slowed the Jeep and turned off the engine. There was hardly a sound. The ocean was far behind them and except for an occasional breeze that moved the bushes and rustled the branches and leaves, it was very quiet.

" C'mon, let's have a look," Byron said as he signaled Chris to join him.

GULLS

He took a note pad from the shelf in front of Chris and flipped it open to the first page that didn't have any writing. Chris saw this stuff on television. He remembered seeing scientists making notes in books on the wildlife television programs. He thought to himself, that he was on a real expedition.

Chris followed close behind Byron as they walked through the sea grass. They came upon a clump of reeds. Something flew away as they approached. It was a small bird.

" Shhhhh. Over here," Byron said as he walked slowly to the tall stalks of grass. He took his right hand and pushed aside the grass. There in the sand was the nest of puffins that he checked each week. The eggs still had not hatched.

" What are they?" Chris asked.

" Puffins. Have you ever seen one?"

" No. Don't think I know what they are."

" They're small birds about this tall," he said as he held his hands showing the size of the birds.

" They have curved beaks. Like this."

Byron took a stick from under the bush and carefully drew a simple picture in the sand. He signaled the shape of the beak, using his hand over his nose.

" When'll they hatch?"Chris asked as he stooped over the nest.

" Well, they should've hatched by now. I guess it'll be soon, maybe today."

Byron was careful not to disturb the nest. He made some notes in his book and they returned to the Jeep.

" Where we goin' now?"

" We have a lot more to find," Byron answered as he finished making some notes in the book.

They drove through the brush and over the dunes checking on more nests. Soon they came upon a gull nest. The gull was quick to leave as they approached.

" Look !" Chris yelled.

" I see it. It won't bother us," Byron said as he turned off the engine. In his mind, he wondered if the gull would leave them alone. He watched as it flew in a few circles overhead and then left the area.

" C'mon let's have a look."

" You sure he won't be back?" Chris asked.

" Don't think so. Besides, I've got this."

Byron slapped the pistol that he was wearing with his hand. It made Chris feel a little more at ease, knowing that Byron could shoot the gulls if they would attack. Chris was hesitant to get out of the Jeep at first, but still, he didn't want to stay there by himself while Byron checked on the nest. Soon Byron finished the examination. He looked all around the area and didn't see anything out of the ordinary, so he returned again to the Jeep with Chris.

" Let's go," he said as he turned the key.

The starter turned very slowly. Then, as though there was no power left, it just stopped.

" Shit," Byron said in a whisper.

" 'We stuck out here?" Chris asked.

" No. we'll be all right. It'll start."

Again, he tried to start it. There wasn't a sound from the starter. Byron reached down and turned on the radio. There wasn't a sound from it either. Then, he hit the center of the steering wheel with the heel of his hand. Not a sound. The horn would not work either. There they sat, in the middle of the bird sanctuary alone. A mile and a half in all directions - from anything.

" I don't want to walk out here," Chris said.

" Let's let it sit here a minute, then we'll try it again. Want a Coke?"

" Okay." Chris said nervously.

" It'll be fine. Don't worry," Byron tried to assure him.

As Byron turned to the rear seat, Chris noticed the gull returning to the nest.

" Look !" Chris said as he pointed to it.

Byron turned forward, watching as the gull circled and swooped down into the tall grass. It had returned to the nest.

"You see. It'll be fine. Stop worrying," Byron told him.

" Here."

As Chris sipped the coke from the can, he watched the sky for any sign of more gulls. He remembered too clearly, the attack on Erica.

Kaaaa Ka Ka Kah Kah Kah Ka Ka

Byron and Chris listened to the sound of the gull as it called out from the beach grass. They looked at each other. Then, Byron tried again to start the Jeep. The tension on the key in the ignition pushed against his fingers as he turned the key to the right. Still, not a sound or a motion from the starter.

Ka Ka ka Kah Kah

Soon, the gull on the nest was joined by another that was circling over the Jeep. Chris hoped that the sound that he heard from the gull wasn't some sort of cry for help and that they were going to come from all over the island.

" Will the radio work?" he asked Byron.

" No. Nothing will work."

" What'll we do now?"

" Let me take a look. Maybe it's a loose wire or something."

Byron got out and lifted the hood. After bracing it with the steel rod, he looked around for a loose connection. There didn't seem to be anything wrong. He unscrewed the six plastic lids on the battery and found that it was bone dry.

" Here's the trouble. The batteries dead. No water in it."

" What'll we do now?" Chris asked while watching the other birds.

" We'll have to walk. We can walk that way to the beach and someone will pick us up. Byron pointed to the tall bayberry bushes. It looked like a jungle. The branches were long and thick and the leaves were thick-set and dense. They're a lot of fisherman out here. They drive along the beach all the time."

" But, what if?"Chris said in almost a panic.

" We'll be all right. Remember, I have this," Byron said as he pointed to the pistol strapped to his side.

" You don't have enough bullets," Chris said.

If they could only have seen over the tops of the bayberry bushes, they would have seen that they were only a few hundred yards from the mountain of shells and the thousands of gulls.

GULLS

The driver of the dozer, was slumped against the seat. The hot summer air drifted across him, and the gulls stood all around the bulldozer waiting for the driver to push a fresh food supply for them. Occasionally, a few terns and albatross would fly in tight circles and then land joining the others. The driver had fallen asleep, lulled by the sound of the gulls and the hot breeze.

Byron tried one more time to start the Jeep. There was nothing happening.

" C'mon ! C'mon !" he begged the engine.

" We'll have to walk," Byron said as he gave the ignition one last try.

" No. We can't. They'll get us."

" I told you, Chris, everything will be all right. The gulls won't bother us.

There aren't even any here. Just the few that we saw. Stop worrying."

" But what if they get us. More will come, just like they did to Erica. They'll kill us."

" I'll shoot them. I told you that. And, I might say, I'm a pretty damned good shot."

Chris sat quietly for a second or two, before he went into an outbreak of tears and sobbing.

" They got Erica! They'll get us, I know it."

" Look, Chris. We can't stay here all day. If they are going to attack, they could just as well get us here. We have to try and get to the beach. I promise you, it will be okay. C'mon stop crying."

After a few more minutes of sobbing, Chris finally agreed to walk with Byron to the beach.

＊

When Marina and David arrived at the hospital, they were met by the nurse that had been taking care of Erica.

" She's ready to go home," the nurse said as she walked with them to Erica's room.

"Well, we're ready to take her home," David replied.

Erica was already seated in the wheelchair. Like every hospital, it was policy that the person would have to be wheeled to the main door. David was glad to push the chair to the elevator.

" Is Chris downstairs?" Erica asked.

" No. Chris is out on the island with Byron Jackson. You remember, the man that works for the national wildlife preservation. The man that's studying birds."

" Oh, right. But when will Chris be home?"

" David, why don't you wait here with Erica while I go to a phone and call Byron? I'll tell him that we are on our way, and that way he'll be there when we get back."

" There. There's a phone in there," David told her, pointing to the waiting room at the end of the hall.

Marina opened her purse and found the card that Byron had given her at the house. After fishing around for a quarter, she slid it into the slot and pushed the numbers that she read on the card.

" Wildlife, Rick speaking."

" This is Marina Spencer. Byron Jackson gave me this number. He said that you could patch me through to him."

"Yes, ma'am. Hold on one second while I call him"

Rick pushed the appropriate keys on the computer keyboard, and also put on a pin microphone headset.

"Unit one. This is base, over."

He waited for a second and then repeated the message.

"Unit one. This is base. Do you read me, over?"

He held his hand over his right ear and listened for the sound of Byron's voice to return to him.

"Unit one, Byron. Do you read me, over."

Still there was no answer. Marina couldn't hear his calls to Byron. Shortly, he pressed the computer keyboard again and he was connected to Marina.

"Ma'am, there's no answer from the Jeep. Could be that Byron is out of his Jeep for a minute. Do you want to hold on and I'll try him again."

"Do you know where they are?" Marina asked.

"They, ma'am? Byron is checking on nests at the north end of the island. He's by himself, I think."

"No. He took my son with him,"Marina told him.

"I didn't know that, ma'am. Do you want to hold and I'll try again?"

"When did you hear from him last?" Marina asked beginning to worry.

"Well, I didn't. Byron doesn't usually call in unless he needs something. He makes the rounds and then returns to the office. Sometimes I don't see him until the end of the day."

Marina watched David standing at the elevator with Erica seated in the wheelchair. She took a deep breath and then continued to question Rick.

" Is there any way that you can get in touch with him?"

" No, ma'am. Not unless he calls in to me. Or if we drive out there and look for him. I'm sure that he's just checking on one of the sites. Do you want to wait a second? I'll try him again."

" Okay, I'll wait."

" Unit one. Hey, Byron, where you be, man?"Rick asked hoping for a response.

Still the radio was silent.

" Ma'am? There's still no answer. Why don't I keep trying and I'll call you. Give me your number."

" I'll be at five five five, six one one four in a few minutes.

I'm at the hospital in Atlantic City right now. We're going to the Rutledge Place from here. We should be there soon."

" Okay. I'll keep trying and call you there. If I get through, what do you want me to tell Byron.?"

" Tell him to bring Chris to the house right away."

" Yes, ma'am."

Marina thanked Rick, and then placed the receiver back on the cradle. She stood for a second, thinking to herself that it may have been a bad idea to let Chris go along with Byron in the first place. Returning to the elevator, she explained the situation to David.

" Rick is probably right. We'll try to call again when we get home, if Rick hasn't already gotten in touch with Kathleen. They're probably going to be there when we get there. Don't worry, Marina. They're okay."

GULLS

✳

As the elevator was returning with the Spencer's to the ground level of the hospital, Byron and Chris began their walk to the beach.

" Sure is thick," Chris said as he pushed aside the long branches.

" We'll just weave in and out of this stuff and soon We'll be at the beach."

Soon, Byron caught a whiff of the decaying clams from the stockpile as the breeze changed direction. He knew instantly that they were close to the mountain of shell.

"What's that smell? It stinks," Chris said while holding his nose with his fingers.

" Clam shells," Byron told him. " The wind changed direction. It's bringing the smell from the bay. It'll be okay. The wind will change again, and you won't have to smell it."

" Makes me sick. I think I'm going to puke," Chris said while squeezing his nostrils.

Byron didn't want to tell Chris about the gulls at the mountain of shells and the fact that they were probably closer to them than he would have liked. He thought that would make him even more scared than he already was.

" Stay closer to me," he told Chris as he walked around the bayberry bushes.

" I'm trying," Chris told him as he ducked under a long branch.

" Here," Byron said

as he put his size twelve foot on a long branch, holding it down onto the sand so that Chris could pass over it.

ka ka ka kah kah kah ka ka ka

The gulls unmistakable calls could be heard from the dunes.

" Do you hear them?" Chris asked.

" Stay closer," he told Chris as he continued walking.

As they weaved in and out of the bushes they became closer to the gulls. On top of the dozer, the driver continued sleeping. The gulls stood in the sand.

ka ka aka ka ka kaaaa kah kah kahh ka ka

" We getting near the beach?" Chris asked.

" Soon," Byron told him. " I can hear the ocean," he said even though he couldn't hear it at all. Byron wanted to give Chris some hope that they would be there soon.

Suddenly, Byron pushed aside some branches and in the opening in front of him, he saw about a dozen of them standing in the sand. He quickly backed away.

" What's wrong?" Chris asked as he all but ran into Byron's back.

" Wait. Let's go this way,"Byron suggested.

Byron backtracked and then took another opening in the bushes. Again, he came upon some more gulls.

Byron found himself also getting scared. The hairs on his arm raised up when he saw the gulls. He knew that he couldn't have Chris go hysterical in fear of an attack. He turned to Chris.

" Chris, listen to me," he said as he crouched down. He was almost whispering to Chris.

GULLS

" What?" Chris asked.

" Look, there are some gulls in there, lots of them but they won't hurt you...I promise."

Just then, Chris took a deep breath. Byron knew that he was going to scream, so he placed his hand over Chris' mouth.

" Don't scream. You'll scare them. Now, listen to me. We can walk though there if we go slow and if we are quiet and don't scare them."

" How many are there?" Chris asked in a whisper.

" Many. Lots," Byron told him.

" Can you shoot them?"

" No. There are too many of them. If we walk slow and if we're quiet, we can just walk past them."

The afternoon sun shone down on the two of them. It was hot and the odor from the mountain grew stronger.

*

As soon as David, Marina, and Erica got settled in the house, Marina asked Kathleen if there had been any calls.

" No, ma'am. Nothin' this mornin'," she answered.

Marina took the card from her purse and went to the phone. While she stared out at the blue ocean and at the stretch of beach that was covered with swimmers that were now laying in the sun, she waited for Rick to answer.

" Wildlife. Rick Wiley speaking."

" Hello, Rick, this is Marina Spencer. Has Byron called in yet?"

" No, ma'am. He hasn't. Let me try again."

Rick tried three or four times to reach Byron but the radio stayed silent. "Tell ya what, Mrs. Spencer," Rick said.
"I'll jump into my Jeep and take a ride out there. I'll find them and call you."

" Thank you. Should I go with you, Rick?"

" No. That's okay. I won't be too long. I'll call you."

When Rick disconnected Marina from the phone line, he pressed the keyboard again.

" Unit one. This is base," he said over and over again.

Damn it, Byron. Where in the hell are you? he said in a whisper to the empty room.

✳

" I don't want to do it," Chris told Byron. "I'm scared."

" We have to. Damn it, Chris. It's the only way out of here. Listen to me," he pleaded with Chris. " Just walk slow and quiet, and we can do it."

They began their trek through the opening in the bushes. Byron held down another branch with his foot and allowed Chris to pass by him. In the opening, the gulls stood staring in all directions. When they saw

GULLS

Chris enter the thoroughfare leading to the beach, the gulls hopped away from the entrance. Byron was careful to allow the branch to return to close the entrance without startling the gulls.

Suddenly, the gull in the center of the group called out, ka ka ka kah kah kah ka ka ka

It continued throwing its head back as it cried out.
kaaa ka ka ka ka ka

Chris was scared. He stood in the center of the group as the gulls closed around his feet. Byron stood directly behind him. They were all around him.

" Go ahead, over there," Byron whispered, as he pointed to the opening on the other side of the sandy oasis.

Chris began walking slowly again. His feet slid along the ground, slightly off the sand, as he moved through the gulls. They parted in front of him reluctantly. It seemed that this was their territory and they felt the intruders should wait for them to move. A few gulls refused to give way to Chris and Byron. As they reached the opening, Chris ducked his head under some tall branches and walked through the long sandy path under the bushes to the next opening. Suddenly, Chris stopped and then turned to run away. He ran directly into Byron.

"I'm not going in there," he said.

" Why? C'mon Chris, we're almost there. You can do it."

*

Rick grabbed the keys to the Jeep and took off running through his office to the door. Without hesitation, he flung it open and ran to the Jeep. Even before his body was inside and seated, he had the key in the ignition. It started quickly and he slapped it into low gear and pulled away from the building. Rick paid no attention to the speed limit as he raced to the north along Atlantic Boulevard. Once reaching the beginning of the wildlife preserve, he down-shifted the Jeep and entered the sanctuary by way of the small opening in the sand dune beside the public parking lot. He stopped the Jeep for a minute and tried to remember the route that Byron took to make the rounds of the sanctuary. Remembering that Byron always ended up at the north end of the island and that he always returned by driving along the surf, Rick turned the Jeep toward the hard surface of the beach. The two red lights were spinning inside the plastic domes that protected the revolving reflectors. He felt in his gut that something was wrong. It made him push the gas pedal down further. The Jeep moved faster. Byron and Rick were the only two on duty and that left no one back at the office should someone call.

Marina returned to the living room after getting Erica settled in. She was stretched across the sofa in the recreation room, watching television. Marina could feel it. The instinctive unrest of her consciousness. She knew that something was wrong.

Why didn't they hear from Byron. It was stupid, she thought, to let Chris go with him. Marina knew that she couldn't handle another disaster. Outside the plate glass windows of the Rutledge Place, there was no sign of gulls. She walked closer to the glass and looked up and down the beach. She saw nothing. Straining her eyes, she noticed some sandpipers scattered along the beach in front of the house, but there were no gulls anywhere. That made her feel a little better. She did not know that they had scraped the beach and took the clam shells from the night's tide to the north end. She did not know that Chris was now only a few yards from thousands of gulls. But Marina knew that something was wrong.

" C'mon," Byron told Chris.

In the opening in the bayberry bushes, there were hundreds of gulls, standing in the sand. None were flying around. Byron thought that it was unusual for that many gulls to remain still, especially at this time of day, when they are usually the most active.

Chris must be scared to death, he thought. Now he walked close to Byron as they crept through the field of birds. He felt they would never get through this without the gulls taking to the air. Byron remembered the tracks in the sand from the attacks on Leslie. Just because they were not flying didn't mean that they were not capable of attack from the ground. But they seemed docile enough.

Meanwhile, Rick continued speeding along the beach, trying to reach the end of the island as fast as he could.

" Careful," Byron whispered to Chris as they approached the other side of the opening.

" Listen !" Chris whispered.

He could hear the ocean breakers and they knew they were almost there. Suddenly, they heard the sound of a diesel engine starting. The bulldozer came alive. From the sound of it, it couldn't be more than fifty feet from them. All at once, the gulls took to the air.

ka ka ka ka ka

Byron and Chris couldn't see in front of them because there were so many gulls swirling around.

" Run !" Byron screamed to Chris.

They both broke out into a gallop as they rushed through the bushes. Overhead, the gulls swirled and dived. All at once they all took to the air. The sound from the dozer grew louder as it approached the mountain of shells.

From the beach, Rick could see hundreds of gulls lift from the bayberry bushes. Without hesitation, he turned the Jeep toward them. He felt certain that they were swirling around Byron and Chris. Rick was afraid of what he might see when he approached the gulls. From where he was, he could not see the mountain of sea shells. The cloud of gulls grew bigger as Rick sped across the soft sand.

" Run !" Chris yelled to Byron.

The branches slapped Byron in the face as Chris ran through them. There was no time to worry about the branches. Instead, he followed Chris as he ran faster through the low openings in the bushes. Byron reached for the pistol that he had strapped in the leather case on his side. Knowing that it wouldn't do much good, he tried while running, to unfasten the flap. Chris was clear of the bayberry bushes and started up the first of the sand dunes that lined the beach. Byron was directly behind him.

" Hurry !" Byron called out.

Reaching the top of the sand dune, they saw Rick approaching from the beach with the red light flashing. It never looked so good, Byron thought to himself, as they ran down the other side of the dunes.

" Get in !" Rick yelled out to them.

Byron stumbled and slid down the sand dune as he followed Chris to the Jeep. They jumped in and Rick continued the circle in the sand. Overhead, the gulls continued to swirl.

" Wait !" Byron called out.

Rick slowed the Jeep and continued the circle until they were facing the gulls again. The gulls hovered and circled the mountain of shells. A new supply of food was exposed from the blade of the bulldozer. Byron realized that there was no attack. There was not going to be an attack. The gulls did not do anything unusual. Others flew directly over them as they sat in the Jeep.

" There's nothing wrong with them," Byron said.

" Nothing wrong," Chris added.

" No. Look. They're just feeding. C'mon lets get out of here."

Rick started the Jeep moving again and they went speeding in the direction of the Rutledge Place.

CHAPTER FOURTEEN:
Why Are They Doing This?

At the Rutledge Place, Marina stood in front of the tall windows. Why did I ever come to this place she asked herself. Outside, it looked so serene, so calm, quiet, and beautiful. The ocean reflected the bright sunlight and the tips of the ocean white caps sparkled like tiny gems scattered across the blue-grey vastness. This place that David had loved so much as a child was nothing more than a nightmare for Marina. Why are they doing this to us, she questioned? Why are they torturing us?

She walked over to the large sculpture and felt the smoothness of the wood with her slender fingers. The gulls, as inanimate as they were in this carving of wood, evoked a feeling of intimidation as Marina looked at the carved eyes in the piece. Quickly, she took her hand away from the sculpture as though it held some mystical power and she feared it possessed something that could take over her soul.

GULLS

David tried to call Rick again. There was no answer.

" Maybe I should go out there," He said.

" I don't know. I guess," Marina replied.

Just then, Marina saw the Jeep speeding in the direction of the Rutledge Place. The red lights were flashing as it made it way across the wet sand.

" Wait! Look at this,"Marina said as she saw the Jeep.

David crossed the room and together they watched the Jeep approach the house. Marina ran to the door and David was right with her.

" Mom !" Chris yelled from the Jeep.

" Mom! Dad! You should have seen them! There were millions of them!"

Byron jumped from the Jeep before it was stopped. Chris followed behind him.

"Mister Spencer, Mrs. Spencer," Byron said as he approached them. " Nothing happened. We broke down and had to walk to the beach. It's fine, believe me."

" Tell them about the gulls," Chris added.

" You said he would be all right," Marina said.

" We were all right. We were just too close to where the gulls are being fed. We did have to walk through them on our way to the beach, but they were fine...really."

Marina invited them in. In the kitchen, they stood around the counter, talking about the event.

" I don't understand why they didn't attack us. I mean, we were in the middle of hundreds of them,"Byron said.

Marina shuddered at the thought that Christopher was in such a precarious position.

" The damned battery went dead in the Jeep and we found ourselves in the middle of hundreds of them," Byron continued telling them.

Kathleen had the television on in the corner of the counter.

" Some of the countries' most popular beaches may be closed for this Labor Day weekend," the announcer said. " Gull attacks have continued to take place on beaches both here in the U.S. and also on beaches in Europe and Australia. No one at this time is able to explain the vicious behavior of some of these birds. We will have a special broadcast tonight at nine o'clock eastern, eight o'clock central time," he concluded.

" I can't believe this," Byron continued. " I mean, we were in the middle of them and nothing happened. Anyway, I'm sorry about all this. I didn't mean to frighten you."

" It was awesome," Chris added like a small boy bragging - acting as if he wasn't scared.

Byron and Rick left to return to the wildlife headquarters. As soon as they got back, Byron went to the bookshelf and began scanning though his many books for an answer to this dilemma.

Half the night, he spent studying. He fell asleep on the sofa with a book in his hands. The next morning, he left for some coffee and brought some doughnuts back with him. He turned on the morning news program while he heated his old coffee in the microwave.

GULLS

" ... now here's a bottle of a popular body oil made by a leading manufacturer of lotions," the guest said to the morning news host. "Unlike the other pesticides, this, according to the manufacturer, does not contain any pesticides."

Displayed in front of the guest was an assortment of insect repellents. Byron had tuned in toward the end of the segment but he supposed that the ten-minute segment had been spent on bug sprays.

" If there aren't any insecticides in the oil, then how does it manage to repel bugs?" the host asked.

" No one really knows. We can only surmise that it mixes with your body chemistry and the odor alone is enough to keep the bugs away," he continued. " But using this stuff in full strength seems to work."

The show didn't offer much more so Byron turned off the television. Taking his coffee with him, he got into Rick's Jeep and headed for the Rutledge Place.

When he arrived Marina was packing the family's things for the trip back to Kansas. She was careful to make certain that all the clothes were clean when she repacked them in to the suitcases. She heard the same morning news program and the report on the bug sprays. The doorbell rang and Kathleen opened the door.

" Why, yes, sir. Let me get her. Wait in here," she said to Byron.

Marina placed the last item into the small suitcase and started down the steps to meet Byron.

" Good morning, Byron," she said.

" Mornin', ma'am. I was just wondering, could I ask you a question?"

" Sure. Go ahead."

" Was Erica wearing any of that popular ...."

" Was Erica wearing Skin-So-Smooth?" Marina interrupted. " I saw the same thing this morning on TV. No. She wasn't wearing any of it. I can't stand the odor of the stuff in full strength."

" Damn. I just thought ..." Byron continued.

" No. Erica wasn't wearing it. It was early in the day. To tell you the truth, Byron, I didn't think anything about bug spray or anything. I have a neighbor that uses that stuff for bug repellent and I can tell you this, if I was a bug, I wouldn't go near her."

" Well, thank you, Mrs. Spencer."

" You're welcome, Byron," Marina answered. " Oh, we're leaving the island tonight. Going back to Kansas."

" Can I say goodbye to Chris?"

" No. Sorry. Chris is out with his dad, but they should be back in an hour or so if you'd like to stop back?"

" Can't," Byron said. " I have to make the island rounds and help Rick start the Jeep from yesterday. I could stop later this afternoon if that would be okay?"

" Certainly. Anytime will be fine."

Marina returned to packing the suitcases as Kathleen brought clean clothes from the dryer. Marina was thinking about the morning news program and the oil that was used for bugs. No, she thought, there are millions of people that use the stuff on the beach. The report told her that. He also said that, if that was the case, there would be far more attacks.

GULLS

Byron drove along the beach, watching the people sunbathing on their blankets and towels. He stopped the Jeep and got out to walk. As he walked through the people, he glanced at the things that they had lying on the beach chairs and towels. He was looking for the popular product that was the focus of the morning news show. Finally, he came upon three girls lying face down on their blankets with their bathing suit tops undone. Each was lathered with suntan lotion.

" Excuse me," he said. " Is this yours?" he asked them as he picked up the bottle of Skin-So-Smooth.

" Yeah, it's mine," one girl answered as she hooked her top with the latch in the middle of her back.

" You using it now?" he asked.

" Sure am. It keeps the beach flies from eating us up."

The three girls were in their mid-twenties. Each had a perfect suntan. Byron summarized that they must have been on the beach for many days to get a suntan that dark.

" Have you been using this all week?" he asked them.

" Yes. We always use it,"two of the girls answered in unison.

" Thanks," Byron said as he walked on to the next group.

Byron estimated that about one out of every six people was using the oil to repel the bugs. He stopped and asked approximately twenty people the same question. They all had been using the oil for a number of years. Byron thought to himself that there must be a connection somewhere.

Returning to his Jeep, he heard Rick calling on the radio.

" Base to unit one. Do you copy, over."

" Unit one here. Go ahead, Rick."

" There's been another attack over on the bay side."

" I don't believe it," Byron said. " How bad?"

" Don't know. The attack was on the Eighteenth Street pier."

" Okay, I'm going over there. Call ya later," Byron told him.

The sun was hot but the morning air felt good to Byron as he drove away from the hot sand and beach. Reaching the Eighteenth Street pier, Byron parked the Jeep and walked to the dock. The lifeguard on duty at this station was telling a group of young girls about the attack. Byron listened in on the conversation.

" Yeah, you should have seen it. Christ, they came from all over," the lifeguard told them. " Before we could get to her, they were all over her."

" Where was she?" Byron asked the lifeguard.

" She was out there. In a canoe, feeding the freakin things."

Byron could tell that the lifeguard thought himself a hero and was going to boast the story all day to anyone who would listen.

" Do you know what she was feeding them?" Byron asked.

" No idea," the guard replied. " I saw her throwing something into the air and they came from all over. I blew this whistle until I was blue, but she didn't stop."

" Where is she now?"

GULLS

" She went with the ambulance people. I don't think she was hurt all that bad," he told Byron. " Looked like she just has a few bites on her shoulders."

" Where's the canoe she was using?"

" Over there," a young girl said as she pointed. " C'mon I'll show you."

Byron and the girl went to the pier next to the swimming area. Bobbing in the water was the canoe that the girl had taken out into deeper water to feed the gulls. Byron looked all through the boat. Under the seat of the canoe he found a towel. The girl had stuffed it there after it had gotten wet. It was rolled up in a tight roll, like swimmers always do to carry their towel under their arm. Byron took it from under the seat and was careful to roll it open across the seat of the canoe. Inside the towel was a small plastic container. It was bright red. Byron had seen these on the beach. They were used for carrying anything small. Inside, she had put some change.

There was sixty cents in change and three one dollar bills rolled-up. He looked into the small container and saw a ring. Dumping the container over again, into his hand, it revealed a class ring. Byron looked at the sides of the gold and read the inscription "Lane High School" also the numbers on one side, "One Nine" and on the other " nine two". He continued looking carefully in the canoe for anything else. In the corner against a support bar, he found a wet morsel of a tortilla chip. He carefully took it from against the rail and put into the palm of his left hand. Why are these things doing this, he thought to himself. As he rubbed the chip with his index finger, he was thinking of the attack on Erica. The attack on Leslie. Could this chip have anything to do with the behavior of these gulls? No, he thought, as he dropped his hand into the dark and cool bay water. The chip stayed on the surface and Byron could see the multi-colored slick of oil from the chip spread on the water. As the oil from the chip dispersed, something came to the surface and ate the morsels. In seconds, the few pieces disappeared.

" What are you looking for?" the young girl asked him.

" Don't know. I guess I'm looking for anything. I'm looking for anything that will give me a clue."

" You should have seen them," the girl said. " They came from out of nowhere. In seconds, there were gulls all over her. Next thing we knew, we could hear her screaming. Then she dove off the canoe into the water. The lifeguards were already on their way out to her. But she never came up until she reached the pier. I couldn't swim that far under water, believe me."

" How bad was she hurt?" Byron asked.

" I don't think she was hurt too bad. She was screaming at the top of her lungs when she came out of the water, but I think I would too. Somebody called for the ambulance and they took her away in it. I couldn't see how much she was hurt 'cause there were so many kids hanging around her."

" Did you know her?" Byron asked.

" No. Not really. I have seen her here before. I think she's down here for Labor Day vacation."

" Thanks," Byron ended.

He returned to the Jeep and decided to head for the rescue squad headquarters a few blocks away. They may have taken her to the hospital, but maybe he could find out something from the paramedics.

" Unit one to base, over."

" Go ahead, Byron," the voice answered.

" Rick, do you know any more about the girl in the attack?"

" No," Rick answered. "I know about as much as you do. I first heard about it on the scanner but their weren't any details.

...Hey, Byron, they're not taking her to the hospital. That much I heard. I think she's at the fire house,"Rick concluded.

" I'm headed there now," Byron answered. " Talk to ya later."

" Okay, unit one. Over and out."

Byron turned onto the apron of the fire house parking area anxious to talk to the girl. The ambulance was parked at the door and two island police cars were parked with their lights still flashing. Inside, they were treating the girl.

"We'd better take her," the one paramedic suggested.

" Okay, let's go," said the other.

" No. I'm fine," the girl said in a loud voice.

" But you could have a serious infection from them," the paramedic told her.

Byron stood in the background listening to the bickering between the girl and the paramedics concerning her safety. Where are her parents he thought to himself?

" I'll be fine, damn it. Leave me alone," she demanded.

Byron thought that she must not have been hurt too badly, if they had not already taken her to the hospital. From what he could see, she was fine. One of the paramedics was applying something on her left shoulder as she sat on a stainless steel table. She was holding the top to her bathing suit against her chest with her right hand as the medic carefully looked at the rest of her shoulders. There was no blood and the paramedic took her fingers and felt the girl's skin along her left arm, looking for punctures.

" Are you sure they didn't get you there?" the paramedic asked.

" I'm sure. Look," she said as she dropped her bathing suit top away from her breasts and then quickly tried to cover herself again.

" I'm fine. Let me get out of here," she pleaded again.

In the confusion of trying to plead her case and to be released, she did not realize that she was still exposing her left breast to everyone in the room.

" Here. Cover yourself," a female paramedic said, as she gave the girl a white towel from the ambulance.

It was easy to see that she was aggravated. But, much to her disapproval, after some discussion, they still decided to take her to the hospital. Byron watched as they walked with her to the door. He didn't see any signs of blood. He did notice that she had some bandages on her hands and some gauze on her thigh. It was clear to Byron that he wouldn't be able to talk to her until she got to the hospital.

Byron looked at his watch. It was almost two in the afternoon. After leaving from the fire house, he turned on Brigantine Boulevard and headed in the direction of the Rutledge Place. He hoped to see Chris and maybe talk to Erica before they left.

Marina and David were arguing in the bedroom about leaving. David couldn't get a flight out of Philadelphia until early the next morning. Not soon enough to suit Marina.

" I don't care. We'll stay in the city tonight. But I'm getting the hell out of here. I don't want to stay another minute more than I have to on this island."

" Please, Marina. What difference would staying here one more night make?"

" How can you say that to me, David?" Marina yelled. " I mean look, we can't go out to the beach. The damned gulls could return at any time. We shouldn't have come to this place at all."

Chris heard the doorbell ring and invited Byron to come in when he answered it.

" How's your sister doing?" Byron asked.

" Fine. She's in the den. Wanna see her?"

" Where's you mom and dad? "

" Upstairs, I'll get them."

Marina and David set their differences aside for a minute as they came down to meet Byron. Marina still wanted to leave the island as soon as she could. David was set on staying just one more night.

" Mister and Mrs. Spencer," Byron said. " I wonder

if I could talk with Erica?" he asked.

"I don't know, Byron. She still is having a problem with the whole thing. Doctor White said that she's to get lots of rest. I'm afraid that talking about the attack could upset her too much," Marina said.

" Okay, then, I was just hoping that Erica might be able to tell me something that I missed. I'm convinced that there's a reason for the gulls behavior. Believe me, Mrs. Spencer, this is not something that gulls do. I mean, look at Chris and myself. We were in the thick of things out on the island and they didn't bother us at all."

" I have been listening to the news," David said. " There isn't anything new about why they're doing this. This TV even gets Europe. The satellite dish pulls in stations from all over the world. I've been scanning all of them, trying to find out anything. I did get one station from somewhere that was reporting on them, but I couldn't understand a damned thing they said."

" I'm trying to put this together on my own," Byron added. "There has got to be a reason."

" Okay," Marina said. " You can talk to her, but not very long. Please, Byron, I don't want her upset."

Erica was lying on the sofa watching television when they entered the room. The wide screen TV filled the far end of the room. It looked like a stadium scoreboard screen that Byron had seen so many times on football games. When Erica heard them coming into the room, she was quick to push the button on the remote control. The six-inch-tall word "Mute" appeared in the corner of the picture. Behind it was a movie Byron, instantly recognized. The picture switched scenes to a space vehicle and there was an explosion with pieces of the computer-animated space craft flying in all directions. Even with no sound coming from the television, Byron's mind replayed the sound in his mind. He had seen every episode of Star Trek over a hundred times, and like every other Trekkie, he would know in a split second exactly which episode and which scene it was.

" Erica," Marina said. " This is Mr. Jackson. He is with the wildlife preserve."

" Hi," Erica said.

Byron was taken aback by the number of wounds that were visible on Erica. He tried not to show that he was looking at them. All over her face and arms were dark, almost black scabs. He could see that Erica was a very beautiful girl. Her long blonde hair looked extremely fine and stretched over her shoulder and lay across the pillow. The dark green color of the sofa and pillows accentuated the bright golden color of her hair. Byron was surprised that Erica still had the bright and beautiful sparkle in her eyes that is most often the expression of a young child. She looked straight into Byron's dark almost black eyes. Instantly, he thought again of how much he wanted to solve this problem. How he wanted more than anything else to find the answer.

" Hi, Erica," he said to her. " How do you feel?"

" I'm okay."

" Erica," he continued. " I'm trying to find out why the gulls are doing this. Do you mind if I ask you a couple of questions?"

" No. Why not? Everybody else has."

" Your mom said you were feeding them."

" Yeah. I was just throwing them some popcorn and then, wham!"

" Did you see any birds other than gulls?"

" No. I don't think so. They all looked like gulls. It happened fast. All of a sudden they knocked me down. I don't remember much after that. I was watching mom in the house. It was hard to see her with all the gulls flying around. Then one of them bit me ... right here," Erica, pointed to her left shoulder at the scar.

"Then wham! Another one got me right here," she said as she placed her finger on her neck. " Then they started biting my hands ... all over."

" When you fell down into the sand, did they bite you on your back?"

" They bit me all over. Like I said, I don't remember much after they first started to bite me."

Byron was convinced that there wasn't much else to tell. Chris wasn't out with Erica on the beach and Byron had already talked with Chris when they were out on the island.

" Chris, you're not still afraid of the gulls, are you?" Byron asked him.

" Yes," Chris was quick to answer.

" We're all afraid of them," Marina added. " I don't care what makes them do it. I don't want to see another sea gull as long as I live. They're disgusting creatures! They're filthy! I don't ever want to see them again, even if it means never coming to the beach."

" They'll find out why they're doing this, Mrs. Spencer," Byron said. " I'm sure it's something strange. Really, they're docile birds. They wouldn't hurt anyone."

"Well, call me when you find out. In the meantime, we're leaving here tomorrow," Marina stated.

" Awe Mom," Chris added.

" Chris, we're leaving in the morning. Early. That's that," Marina insisted as she turned and left the room.

David was somewhat surprised that Marina had made her decision to stay for one more night.

" Well, thank you," Byron said as he stood to leave the room.

In the background, the television was switched to a commercial. Byron watched as the sway of a girls rear end walked the beach. In the background, the ocean sparkled. Quickly, the edit switched again to a sea gull being pushed out into the deep water by the wind. The words "Mute" were still on the screen. Before Byron could ask them to turn on the sound, the TV commercial ended and Star Trek re-run was back on the screen again.

" Goodbye, Chris," Byron said as he walked toward him.

" Bye, Byron," Chris said as he shook Byron's hand.

As Byron walked down the hall with David, Chris yelled out from the den," Byron! See ya ... wouldn't want to be ya!"

✳

CHAPTER FIFTEEN:
On to Something

Byron drove to the jetty at the south end of the island where the inlet leads to the Brigantine Bridge. He had changed from his uniform into his cut-off shorts and t-shirt. Walking along the beach to the rocks he watched as the gulls gathered in the lights above the hotels of Atlantic City, less than a tenth of a mile away. He could see them clearly across the short inlet. It was getting dark and the millions of lights both in, on, and over the hotels made the popular resort look like a fantasy land. People by the thousands were gathered for the entertainment offered by the casinos and the gulls were the farthest thing from their minds. From where he stood, it was both peaceful and serene. He began walking carefully down the rocks to the incoming ocean waves. They slammed against the granite and sprayed a shower of salt water over them.

The tide was receding for another night, working

slowly away from the beach and revealing more of the man made jetty of stones. He looked up at the full moon that was just appearing from the east. Why, he asked himself, did he pick this place to study the birds,to study the gulls? Thinking, wondering, pondering and even guessing the reason for their behavior dominated his thoughts as he made his way to the receding tide. At his feet, the rocks were now ebony with the dark green blanket of sea moss and he knew they would be slippery. Looking down, to carefully and strategically place his bare feet, he marvelled at the thousands of tiny shells that washed their way into the crevices and stuck in shallow pools of salt water. Reaching the end, he found himself standing on a stone peninsula and occasionally, an island of rock in a violent eruption of sea water that rose from the depth of the incoming waves into a geyser of foam.

Standing there, he watched as it approached. Facing the strong sea breeze. It forced its head forward and stretched its wings to the limit. Byron watched as it struggled to stay above him. The air current was too strong and it was forced away, only to return quickly, in brazen determination. It was beautiful. The wingtips were jet-black and the body was as white as snow. The tip of its beak looked as though it had been dipped in india ink. The amber eyes watched Byron as it lowered itself through the rough air to only a few feet in front of him. How could this thing of grace and beauty now carry with it a bounty, Byron thought.

Byron looked directly into the gull's eyes as it approached and landed at his feet. It did not have any fear of the person standing only a few feet away. Sea water sprayed over the rocks and subsided into the cracks and spaces between the rocks.

Byron stooped to get a closer look at the bird. It hopped a few feet and continued staring at him. He studied the sharpness of its beak, something that he had seen many times before, but now it took on a different appearance. Its razor sharp edges capable of severing a human finger with one bite. Suddenly, as though not wanting to reveal any secrets, it leaped into the sea air and cried out, ka ka ka ka kah kah, as it fought the unstable air for more height. Byron watched as it flew in the direction of the night lights of Atlantic City to circle over the hotels.

The grace and beauty of the gull was something that Byron envied. He had always loved the birds. He loved how they had the freedom to rise above the world and escape the maze of man made walls. These particular birds were his favorite. He studied their habits and behavior for years. He marvelled at the comeback of the tern to the east coast. Once, poisoned almost to extinction because of DDT, they have returned to grace the shores of the east coast.

Finally, after more than twenty years, the puffin would flock to the rocks of New England. Children could once again, find laughter in their funnyfaced small friends. Byron knew that when a species vanishes from the earth, it is another warning signal from nature that something is wrong. He knew also that this sudden change in the behavior of the gull was something that man had caused. He vowed to find out just what it was.

As darkness edged its way inland and the pastel colors of the evening disappeared beneath the night sky, Byron returned to the beach from the rocks.

" Unit one, this is base," the voice said.

" Unit one. Damn it, Byron, where the hell are you?" the voice asked.

Byron was still in a slight trance from his walk on the beach.

" Go ahead, Rick," he answered.

" Hey, Mrs. Spencer has been calling here looking for you. She said she's on to something."

" She's on to something?" Byron quizzed.

" Don't know what it is, my man, but she wants to see you at the Rutledge Place, pronto."

" All right, call her. Tell her I'm on my way."

Byron leaped into the Jeep. He didn't slip on his sneakers. Instead, he depressed the clutch with the ball of his bare left foot and pulled the gear shift into low gear. Simultaneously, he let off on the clutch and pushed the gas pedal almost to the floor. The Jeep began throwing sand and the steering wheel pulled to the right as it dug out of the soft sand and began the race to the Rutledge Place. He vectored the steel horse to the harder wet sand as he quickly went through the gears and brought the Jeep to a speed of fifty miles an hour.

As he arrived in front of the Rutledge Place on the beach side, he noticed that there was little different.

There were no additional cars on the brick driveway. The house was lit like an airport. Byron noticed the familiar sphere was missing from the roof.

It took something away from the awesome appearance of the contemporary house, he thought.

"On to something" was going through his mind over and over as he rang the doorbell.

" Evenin', sir," Kathleen said as the door opened, exposing the foyer and the bright lights inside.

" Good evening, Ma'am."

" The Spencer's are in the kitchen," she continued as she let him through.

" Thank you."

Byron made his way down the hall to the large kitchen. Marina, David, Erica and Christopher were seated at the table. David was first to rise from his chair as Byron entered the room.

" You found something?" he asked.

" Well, maybe. Go ahead, show him," Marina instructed Chris.

" Check this out, Byron," Chris said as he showed Byron a plastic bottle of sunscreen.

Byron walked over to the table and took the bottle of "Olana" sunscreen from Chris.

" I don't understand?"

" Smell it," Chris told him.

Byron opened the fliptop plastic lid and placed the container to his nose. He took a small sniff and it smelled good. It also smelled very familiar.

" Smells familiar," he told them.

" Smells like "Blue" perfume, doesn't it?" Marina asked.

" Yeah. Yeah, that's exactly what it smells like."

" Smells like fish to me," Chris exclaimed. " Smells exactly like that stuff that was going to make me puke. It's not real strong but it smells like it to me," he continued.

" Chris was playing with the bottle on the counter this evening. Next thing I know, he's telling me that it smells like dead fish," Marina added.

Byron instantly connected the odor that Chris interpreted as dead fish to the mountain of shells at the north end of the island.

" I'll be damned," he whispered. " This *could* be the answer. It's too late tonight to find out, I suppose. But, I'd be willing to bet that the gulls find this stuff as appealing as food."

"But wait a minute. Chris is the only one that finds this stuff smelling like clams or fish ... even dead fish. Besides, I checked this stuff when I was checking for Skin-So-Smooth. I saw some bottles of the same lotion on the beach and it didn't cause the gulls to attack those people," he continued.

" Wait, check this out," David added.

They all got up from the table and went with Byron to the recreation room. The television was on, but the screen was gray. David was quick to take the remote control and depress the play button. The screen instantly filled with the Star Trek episode that Erica had been watching earlier in the day. Byron recognized it immediately. Soon, within a few seconds, the tape went to a television commercial.

" Be on the lookout ... for the dark long-haired fox,"

the voice said. Byron watched the model walking the beach with the plastic bottle of sunscreen in her hand.

" ... for she is soon becoming the endangered species," the announcer continued.

" Olana's patented fragrances are now a unique blend of sunscreen and perfume. No longer do you have to smell like cocoa oil on the beach. Try any one of twelve designer fragrances of Olana sunscreen."

" I'll be damned," Byron said under his breath.

" Don't you...become one of the endangered species. Protect your skin. Use Olana sun screen," the announcer stated. " In twelve designer fragrances and available in select department stores everywhere," he concluded.

Then the camera backed away from the girl's long hair, her swaying body, and the bottle of sunscreen she was carrying. Written across the television screen were the words " Olana, Paris, France"

David stopped the tape.

" Erica had it on when I let her out to feed the gulls," Marina said. " It was the last thing that I did before she left. I put the lotion on her. Her face, arms, hands, back ... all over her."

" I'm telling you, Byron, its got to be the answer," David said.

"Where did you get this stuff?" Byron asked Marina.

" In Kansas. I had seen the commercial out there. When I went to the mall with my friend, I saw the sun screen on the perfume counter and decided to buy it. I almost didn't, because it costs a fortune."

" That explains why there isn't that much of it on the

beach," Byron added. " I wonder if the girl in the canoe had this on?"

" Probably," David said.

" Is she on the island?" Erica asked.

" I think so," Byron said.

" Can we call her and talk to her?" Marina asked.

" Let me go over to the rescue squad. They should have her address. Then we can talk with her." But, wait a minute. Those two guys that got it out on the boat. I hardly think they were wearing this stuff."

" True, it does seem doubtful. But, hey ... one of their wives could have left it on the boat. You know how it is when you're fishing. A couple of beers and you don't give a damned what you smell like," David said.

" Anybody wanna go with me?" Byron asked.

" Me!" Chris was quick to say.

" Okay with you?" Byron asked David.

" I guess so."

Byron and Chris left immediately. Outside, the cool night air was more refreshing. Especially now, knowing that they might be getting to the reason for the attacks by the gulls. In a few minutes they had the girl's name and address from the rescue squad. Byron had to use an excuse that he was returning the things that she left in the boat earlier that day. With a little persuasion, he had her name and address and was on his way.

He glanced at the name again when he got back into the Jeep. Kristi Lightner, 201 Ninth Street South. When they pulled up in front of the house, he noticed that all the lights were on.

" C'mon Chris, let's go."

Without answering, Chris climbed out of the Jeep and joined Byron as they walked up the sidewalk.

Kristi answered the door. " Hi, I remember you. I saw you at the fire house today, right?"

" Yes, I wanted to talk with you earlier. My name is Byron Jackson and this is Chris."

" Hi, Chris," she said. " Come in. My parents are in the other room."

" Why did you want to see me? Because of the gulls?"

" Yes. I was wondering if you could tell me, were you using sunscreen while you were out on the boat?"

" I was," Kristi answered. " I always use it. I burn easy if I don't use something."

" Tell me, what's the name of the lotion that you use?"

" Oh, wow. It's "Olana." It's real expensive stuff," Kristi told him.

" Can I see it?" Byron asked.

" Sure, wait a minute, I'll get it for you."

Just then, Kristi's parents came in from the recreation room where they had been watching TV. Byron introduced himself and Chris to them and explained who he was and what his job was on the island. Kristi came back into the room with the familiar bottle of lotion.

" Here," she said, handing Byron the bottle.

Instantly, he noticed the name "Blue" written across the front. Just like Erica, she had used the same sunscreen.

" That's it," Chris said eagerly.

" That's what?" Kristi asked.

" We think there might be a connection with this lotion and the gull attacks. Another girl on the island was attacked by the gulls and she was wearing the same lotion...the same scent. We're going to check it out," Byron told her. " But, in the meantime, I wouldn't use this stuff, just to be safe."

" Hey, okay by me. I sure don't want them coming after me again,"Kristin was quick to state.

Byron and Chris spent a little more time with Kristi and her parents but soon left for the Rutledge Place. Upon arriving, they were met by Marina and David. Byron confirmed that the girl on the bay was wearing the same sunscreen.

" I'm going into the city. I want to talk with the coroner about Leslie, the girl that was killed on the north end," he told them.

" Can I go?" Chris was fast to ask.

" No, I don't even know if I can get to talk to him. You better stay here. I'll come over in the morning. We can go out to the beach early and see if this stuff is what is causing it."

Byron, returned to the Jeep and headed toward the island bridge and to Atlantic City. He knew that the coroner's office would more than likely be at the police station, and he was right. He entered the police station through the glass doors. Inside, there was the usual array of wanted posters. He stood there looking for the directions that would show him to the coroner's office. Hopefully, he thought, there would be somebody there tonight. He wondered what would have happened to Leslie's personal property. He decided to check with the desk sergeant and to try and track down her stuff rather than to talk with the coroner.

The sergeant was reluctant to reveal the personal property from the storage room until Byron explained why he needed the information. The sergeant sent someone to storage and instructed them to bring the items to the front desk. As Byron waited, he watched as the police brought in a drunk. Two uniformed police officers helped the drunken old man through the swinging glass doors. He squinted his face as he entered the brightly lit room. All of a sudden, his body went limp, forcing the two police to drag him to the long bench that filled the wall across from the information desk. Without warning, the drunk puked his guts out, causing the two cops to curse at him. Byron hoped that he could look through the personal property in another room.

Shortly, the young rookie returned with the red cooler that Byron remembered from finding her. The small blanket was neatly folded and held the rest of the items on top, with the cooler being the centerpiece.

" May I?" Byron asked.

Seeing her things brought back the memory of discovering her under the jagged branches. Byron took a deep breath and then opened the cooler. There was nothing in it. Her nylon running shorts were folded neatly under it. Byron carefully lifted the cooler and then moved each item from the stack. First, was her bathing suit top. Directly under that was the bottom half of the suit. The color was the most beautiful shade of blue that he had ever seen. He thought, as he removed it from the stack, about how it must have looked on her.

" You're lucky to find these things here. The family was supposed to pick them up yesterday," the officer said.

Byron didn't answer. He continued looking through the items for any sign of the sunscreen.

" Is there anything else?" he asked.

" Wait," the young cop said. " There is something else. This slip has another bin number written on it. I'll get it. Be right back."

Byron carefully replaced the items back to their original folded positions and placed the cooler on top. Shortly, the rookie returned with the black boom-box and a plastic bag containing more items. Byron opened the plastic bag and found the paperback book that she had been reading. He noticed blood stains on some of the pages as he instinctively flipped through them. He felt it ironic that the book was titled "Hunted". There was an inexpensive quartz wrist-watch in the bottom of the bag and a gold chain.

" Is this all?" he asked them.

" Fraid so," the rookie said. " What are you looking for?" he asked.

" Well, suntan lotion," Byron answered.

" No. Don't think so. This is everything that was picked up from the site. Of course, if there was a bot-tle of lotion it could have been missed."

" Thanks," Byron said as he turned to leave the counter. He had gotten halfway to the door when he thought of something.

" Wait !" he called out.

The rookie was stacking the items so that he could return them in one trip to the storage room when he heard Byron call out. Byron went back to the desk and put his hand on the top of the things.

" Can I see something?" he asked the rookie.

" Sure."

Byron held the stack of items with one hand and pulled the small blanket out from under them. He moved it to the side and then, opened the folds to the center. With both hands he lifted the blanket to his face. There. There it was. He instantly recognized the smell of "Blue" perfume.

He closed his eyes and saw in his mind, the girl laying naked on the blanket. He visualized her body forming a mold in the soft sand and the blanket under her. He knew that the odor of the lotion had transferred from her soft skin to the white fabric. Still standing there, with the blanket held to his face and nose, he began to get caught up in remembering the girl that was dead and the lifeless body on the sand.

He also knew that it wasn't their fault. It was something they couldn't help. To the gulls, he thought, this perfume signaled something else. Marina was more than just on to something. She may very well have solved the problem. Carefully, he replaced the blanket on the counter top and refolded it. He did so with the same reverence that the military folds a flag to pay honor at a funeral.

Byron knew that he didn't have to return to the north end of the island and look for the bottle. The message was clear from the smell of the blanket. As he returned to the Jeep and drove through the streets of Atlantic City, he wondered if they could get the word out fast enough to prevent someone else from getting hurt or killed from the gull attacks. As the cool night air blew into the Jeep from over the windshield, Byron felt a new sense of refreshment. When the light of day appeared, they would find out if this was the reason. In the meantime, it would be a long night, and he doubted very much if he would be able to sleep.

When he reached the island, he drove to the north end to find the bottle of lotion. The headlights peered through the mist and he vectored over and around the dunes to the spot where Leslie was killed. As he walked with his flashlight to the opening in the bayberry bushes, his thoughts were on the gruesome night that was now embossed in his mind forever. Tire tracks and footprints were still clearly visible in the sand and he followed them over the sand dune. Walking slowly, he searched the area with the light and found nothing. Without warning, a gull flew in front of the light as it took off from under the bushes and headed directly for him. Instinctively, he covered his face with his hand, but the gull simply vanished into the darkness. Byron felt secure that they had the answer. Morning would tell all, he thought.

From the vast darkness over the bushes, he heard the cry from the startled gull.

kah, kahh, ka, ka, ka.

CHAPTER SIXTEEN:
See Ya'

Byron woke early the next morning. He was up and making coffee long before the first signs of daylight appeared from out at sea. He wanted to be able to meet with the Spencers and find out more about the gulls before they left for Philadelphia. The gulls remained quiet until the break of day. Then, they began the feeding ritual along the beaches. He heard the heavy equipment from the beach as the drivers began moving the sifters and scrappers. Each morning, they traveled across the sand to gather the shells left behind by the tide. From the small house used as their office, Byron could see the beach and the headlights from the heavy equipment. A pickup truck moved slowly along and the man in the truck removed the signs **"Do not feed the gulls"** from the soft sand. Once the equipment passed, another truck would follow and more signs were replaced.

The headlights peered through the morning mist as

the caravan passed in front of the wildlife office. Byron was finishing his first cup of coffee when the phone rang.

" Hello, this is Byron Jackson. Can I help you?" he answered.

" Morning, Byron. This is David Spencer. Were you able to find out anything?"

" Sure did. When can I come over?"

" Now, if you'd like. We're all up. As you know, we're leaving for Kansas today."

" I'll be right over," Byron said as he hung up and left immediately for the Rutledge Place.

Driving from his quarters to the Rutledge Place was easy at that time of morning. No one was out driving yet. As he passed the first of many convenience stores on the way, he noticed the delivery trucks that brought supplies. This wasn't something that Byron had seen too often. Occasionally, when he had been out partying half the night, he returned to the island from the city, in the wee hours. But he always had to weave in and out of traffic, even if it was very late at night. It only took a few minutes to arrive at the Rutledge Place. He thought it was a remarkable house. Even with the curtains closed the light escaping from inside the rooms, illuminated the curtains and added to the already magnificent splendor of it.

Kathleen greeted him at the door and sent him to the kitchen.

" She was wearing the same sunscreen," he said as he walked down the hall.

" I knew it," Marina said.

" What I don't understand is how they can smell the stuff. It's not that strong, and it smells like perfume, a mild one at that," David added.

" Gulls have the most acute sense of smell. They can come from as much as a hundred miles away to an odor. You would be amazed at how strong their sense of smell really is. Even more amazing," Byron continued, "Is that the sea gull has one of the best senses of smell on earth, second only to the shark," he added.

" So when Erica started feeding the gulls, she just attracted them to the odor and to her?" Marina asked.

" When Erica went out on the beach wearing the sunscreen, I guess it was enough to attract them. I think the stuff might have a chemical reaction that may only effect certain people. That could explain why only some people were attacked."

" Let's try it out. I mean, we have to find out." David said.

" We can put some of this stuff on and see what happens." Byron added. "I should be able to get into cover long before I get bit by them."

It was now beginning to get light. The sky over the ocean became gray. Byron knew that the gulls would begin their feeding soon. If he was going to bait them, he would have to drive to the north end of the island, where they would be congregating.

" If Kristi was feeding them out on the bay then I should be able to bait them from out there as well. I don't really want to go out to the shells, where there are thousands."

" When?" David asked.

GULLS

" Hell, let's go now," he answered.

" I'm not going. David, you shouldn't go either."
Marina said.

Erica and Chris both agreed with their mother that
David should not go. But David was dead set on finding out if this was the reason. He became as caught up
in the mystery as Byron had.

" Well, let's go," David replied.

Reaching the Eighteenth Street pier didn't take long.
Byron pulled the Jeep up to the steps of the pier. The
lifeguard stand stood out from the small boats that
were tied up near it. The bay water was as smooth as
glass. The reflections of the small boats and canoes
tied to the pier looked like the familiar paintings that
could be seen in all the gift shops on the island. When
Byron turned off the engine of the Jeep, they both sat
there in the morning stillness.

" Getting second thoughts?" David asked. " You sure
you want to do this?"

" Don't want to. Have to," Byron replied.

They both climbed out of the vehicle and walked
out on to the pier. It was light enough that they could
see well across the bay. A water bird of some kind had
just robbed a fish from the surface of the still water
and the rings from the strike on the surface were still
marking the spot like a bulls-eye in a large dart board.
The bird continued flying across the bay with the
small fish dangling from its beak. Byron noticed the
bird but had no comment for David.

" Let's take this one," Byron said as he pointed to the
small flat-bottom boat.

" How about one with a motor?" David suggested.

" Here's one with an outboard. Let's take this," Byron said.

Byron stepped into the small boat and David untied it from the pier. As the boat moved away from the piling, David jumped in and quickly sat. Byron was already pulling on the rope to start the reluctant engine. The smell of gasoline filled the air as the small engine became flooded. Byron pulled the small plastic button out to choke the engine and pulled on the rope a few more times. By this time, the boat had drifted across to the next pier and banged into a rowboat that was tied there.

" C'mon you sonuva ...." Byron muttered as he yanked on the cord.

Suddenly, the engine coughed and sputtered then finally started running. White smoke filled the space between the piers quickly as Byron pushed the lever mounted to the side of the boat. Moving it slightly forward helped the engine smooth out and the boat began pushing through the dark bay water.

" Let's not go too far," David said as he turned to Byron at the rear of the boat.

" We better go out about a hundred yards or so."

Byron reached what he estimated to be a hundred yards from the pier and he turned around and pushed the off button on the top of the engine. Instantly, the motor stopped, but the small boat continued drifting forward. Byron stood in the boat and removed his shirt. The early morning air was soothing to his already sweating body. His dark skin became shiny from the perspiration that had beaded up on his chest. He took the bottle of sunscreen and squeezed some into his left hand. As he spread it on his right arm it became white like fresh paint.

Rather than rub it into his skin, he switched hands and did the same application to his left arm.

" How much are you going to use?" David asked.

" I don't know. I guess I'll just put some on my shoulders and We'll see what happens."

" It doesn't smell like fish to me," David said. " It smells like a mild perfume, pretty good at that. Christ, Byron, you smell so good I might ask you out."

They had stopped. The water was still and the sky became lighter. Byron estimated that the sun would be up in little more than a half an hour.

" Do you think we should have brought some popcorn or something to attract them with?" David asked.

" Nah, if they come to me with this stuff on and we aren't baiting them with food, that means there's no question that this is the reason. I just can't believe that this scent smells like this to us ... and smells like something else to them."

" Maybe it's like honey to a bee. Maybe they like the smell so much that they can't resist," David added.

The two of them sat in the bay looking around for the first sign of gulls. There was nothing. Not one single gull appeared.

" Think you have enough on?" David asked.

" Here. You want to try?" Byron said as he offered David the bottle.

" No way, that's okay. This is your show."

The sun was beginning to appear over the ocean. The gulls did not show. Byron and David remained in the boat watching the sky like duck hunters on a pond.

" Maybe it doesn't have the same reaction on my skin that it did for the others. Ya know what I'm sayin'? Or maybe this isn't the reason at all. But it's a helluva coincidence if that's the case," Byron said.

" Look! Over there," David called out.

David watched a single gull as it worked its way to the north.

" Nothin' doin'. He's goin' somewhere else. I guess we better give it up," Byron stated in frustration.

" Damn," David replied. "I guess we were wrong."

Byron turned to the engine and began pulling the rope again. After pulling on it from a sitting position, he decided to stand and get a better and stronger pull. The engine refused to come alive.

" All the boats we could have stolen and we pick this one," Byron said quietly.

After a short break to rest, he began pulling the rope again and again. He tried pulling the choke button out and then tried to start it with the button in.

" We outta gas?" David asked.

Byron opened the lid on the small gas tank at the side of the engine.

" Almost, but there is still some in there," Byron answered.

He rocked the boat back and forth by shifting his weight and then tried the starter again. After a half dozen more pulls, the engine came to life, once more belching white smoke that hung close to the water. Byron turned from the engine and sat facing forward along with David. The boat started moving in the direction of the pier. Behind them, the gulls gathered as though they had come from nowhere. They gathered behind the boat and moved closer to Byron and David.

" I don't understand it?" David said as he turned toward Byron in the rear of the boat. "Jesus! Look out he yelled.   Byron instantly turned to see almost thirty sea gulls coming closer to the boat.

" Where the hell did they come from?" Byron yelled as he grabbed his shirt.

As Byron let go of the throttle, the engine quit. The boat slowed and the gulls drew closer. They were within a few feet of Byron when he dove from the boat. David followed into the cold bay water. The gulls hovered for a second and then scattered in all directions.

" Fuck! That was close," David said.

" Too close," Byron muttered as he began swimming to the boat.

They were now only a few feet from the pier, so Byron elected to stay in the water until David could climb into the boat and steer them to the pier. Byron swam alongside until it slowly came to a stop against the first piling.

" Are we safe now?" David asked.

" I think so."

They tied the boat at the first piling and returned to the Jeep.

" Damn! Where the hell did they come from?" Byron asked.

" Beats me," David said. " They came from out of nowhere. God. Can you imagine? Shit, look how fast they can gather when somebody's feeding them on the beach. That stuff must really smell good to them."

" Chris said he thought it smelled like fish to him. I don't see it. Smells like perfume to me."

" Well, I think we know now that it's the culprit," Byron said.

He started the Jeep and they headed for the Rutledge Place.

" I can still smell the stuff," David said.

" Yeah, it's like that skin stuff they use for bugs. It stays on you for a long time."

" You can shower when we get there. Kathleen will dry your things for you," David offered.

As the new day began with the bright sun shining on Brigantine Island, Byron and David worked their way through the early morning traffic to the circle at the entrance to the island. They circled the landmark lighthouse and then turned off onto Atlantic Avenue and continued toward the Rutledge Place. Before this day would be over, they would get the message out and the gull attacks would end. As they made the turn onto Atlantic Avenue, they passed under the canvas sign stretched across the road. It read " Welcome to Brigantine Happy Labor Day Weekend."

When they arrived at the house, Marina had a message for David.

" Suzette called a minute ago," Marina told him "

She's at the hotel and wants you to call her. She said it's important. You're to call her before we leave."

"Thanks, Marina," David said. "We're sure now. You should have seen them. Out of nowhere. Byron damned near got it," he continued. "If he hadn't dove in the water, they'd a got him."

David continued to tell Marina and the kids what had happened as he went to the phone to call Suzette. He stood in the living room with the phone to his ear and his eyes transfixed on the sculpture of the gulls at the other end of the room.

"Hi, Suzette. What's up?"

"Hey, boss. Sorry to bother you this morning, but it seems you're in for a promotion. Doug Porter said that the deal went through on the company here in Atlantic City and you're the guy that's taking over. He wants you to call him this morning. I guess I shouldn't have told you, but he is dead set on you taking the job."

Suzette's voice was filled with excitement for David as she told him of the promotion. Marina and Byron continued talking about the gulls as David listened to Suzette and the news of the promotion. Instantly, David knew that Marina wasn't going to have any part of this promotion. Especially if it meant that they would have to live in Atlantic City, or for that matter, anywhere on the coast. Hell, he thought to himself, she can't wait to get out of here now.

"When's this supposed to happen?" he asked Suzette.

"Now. I think he wants you to stay and then move out here later. David, it's a done deal. You get company perks and all. You better not forget your dear secretary. I love it out here, Boss."

"When you leavin'?" David asked her quietly so that Marina wouldn't hear him.

"Tonight. I have a late flight. Hey, I want to get as much partyin' in as I can."

"I'll call you later, Suzette. Will you be around the hotel?"

"Yes. I'm going to get caught up on some sleep and stay around for most of the day. I got burnt on the beach yesterday, so I thought I would take it easy today."

"I'll call you later then. Oh, thanks, Suzette."

Marina had just finished talking with Byron about the bay incident and had returned to the kitchen. David knew this would mean a huge salary increase for him. Standing in the middle of the Rutledge Place gave him a feeling that he should accept the promotion and stay here.

He reached for the phone again and carefully pushed the numbers nine, one, one.

"Police emergency. Can I help you?" the voice on the other end said.

He handed the phone to Byron. Byron explained the bay scene and the facts about the lotion. He insisted that they get the word to the media. Before he had even finished his conversation with the dispatcher, the first police car pulled into the brick driveway.

Within a few hours, the Rutledge Place was filled with reporters and officials. All of the media that was on the island when they were looking for Leslie were once again back for the news. Outside the house, news vans and television satellite antennas were visible to anyone walking the beach. Before they could send the story out to the world, they would have to talk with the manufacturer of the product in Paris.

The major networks were on hand to find out exactly who they would have to talk with at the manufacturer. After some research, they uncovered the fact that the company was owned by a major perfume manufacturer in New York.

Marina wasn't prepared mentally for all the people that were in the house and outside waiting to talk with them and Byron. By tomorrow morning, the deluge of people would begin arriving for the Labor Day weekend. She knew that no matter what, she would be on the plane with Chris and Erica, bound for Kansas.

" They have agreed to pull the product," someone said from the crowd in the living room.

Lynda Dalton, news correspondent for a Philadelphia newspaper, made the phone call to the manufacturer.

" They're not going to make any appearances on the subject. But they will hold a press conference as soon as they are able to meet with their chemists and attorneys," she added.

The room became noisy as each reporter who had a cellular phone began to call their office with the information. Byron was under the makeshift studio lights and being prepared to be interviewed by the local television station.

Marina and Erica were being interviewed in the corner of the living room by the local newspaper. They asked her and the kids to stand in front of the wooden sculpture for a picture. Flashes of light from strobe units flashed as each photographer took multiple pictures of them. Already, before the interviews were complete, the word was being placed on the wire service .

" We interrupt this program with a special bulletin," the announcer said.

Each television network aired the bulletin at the same time. No network was able to get the edge or the advantage over the others. Simultaneously, the word was going out.

" The manufacturer of "Olana", sunscreen has announced that they are pulling their product from the shelf. It seems that one particular fragrance, the fragrance called "Blue", is responsible for the recent attacks by sea gulls. This behavior has baffled officials and researchers. It has been discovered that the scent of the sunscreen actually attracts the gulls and initiates their aggressive and deadly behavior. The manufacturer has asked that if anyone has purchased the product, return it immediately for a full refund," he continued. "The manufacturer of, Daydream perfumes, has told us that there have only been a few thousand bottles of the product distributed. Daydream Perfumes will withhold shipment of any additional bottles and urges anyone who has the product to return it. We'll have a more complete report on the product and the attacks along with a news conference with the manufacturer, as soon as the information is available," he concluded.

David excused himself from the reporters and slipped into the guest bedroom. Much to his surprise, he was able to place his call to the home office, All that Suzette had told him was true. The company successfully purchased their leading competitor and they wanted David to stay in Atlantic City for an upper level management position. They would purchase his house in Kansas from him and move the entire family to the east. He thanked his boss for the promotion, but said that he would have to discuss it with Marina and the family before making his decision. David didn't know if he could get a decision from Marina before the plane would leave for Kansas from Philadelphia later that day. With a room full of reporters and cameras, he wasn't sure if they would be able to leave today.

In the living room, Byron was being interviewed by the local news reporter for one of the four major networks. He had become a celebrity overnight. As the camera lights projected the heat in his direction, he couldn't help but remember the fear that he had when he saw the gulls heading for him only a few hours earlier.

" I knew there had to be a reason for their attacks," he said to the reporter. "I have been studying birds and gulls almost all my life and knew that this sudden change had to be something strange."

" Did you have any hints that the perfume was the reason?" she asked.

" No. None at all. Chris was the one that stumbled on it. He was the one that said the perfume, to him, smelled like something else. That is what put us on to it. Then we did our own experiment to find out for sure," he continued. " Let me tell you, they apparently love the stuff, because there was no way they were stopping coming after it. If I hadn't dove into the water, they would've had me for breakfast."

The interviewer turned from Byron to face the camera.

" There you have it. What smells like one thing to us may very well smell like something else to other things. We know that certain products keep bugs away, although they have no repellents. This product attracts gulls. The ramifications of the scent, however, are a fatal attraction," she said. " This is Karen Holiday for Channel Six Eye-watch News," she concluded.

CHAPTER SEVENTEEN:

Kansas or Not?

" Mom," Erica said to Marina. " Dad wants to talk to you. He's up in the bedroom."

" Be right there," Marina told her as she turned from the last of the reporters leaving the house. Kathleen was trying to keep up with the people that were coming and going from the house and Chris was seated with Byron. By now, they were exhausted from answering a million questions from the reporters. There would be more to come. Byron had been invited to go to New York in the morning for a network morning news program and he had accepted. David had also been asked if Chris could appear with Byron on the news show.

When Marina reached the top of the stairs, she saw David staring at the boarded-up hole in the ceiling.

" Mark is going to just love that," Marina said as she went to him.

" Yeah, We'll pay for it, I guess. I was a helluva shot though, wasn't I?"

GULLS

" You hit the skylight and you got the damned gull out. That's all I was looking for."

" Marina, I've been offered a promotion with the company. It means a lot more money and it means that I'll be a vice-president,"he said candidly.

" What's the catch, David? You have this doubt in your voice. I can always tell when you're not sure about something."

" The catch, Marina, is they want me to stay here in Atlantic City."

" No! No way. I'm out of here with the kids, David. I can't trust those things. Even if we lived inland, I would worry constantly about them. Damn it," she continued, "The next thing you know, they'll take a liking to underarm deodorant or something. No. I'm not staying."

" Marina, this whole thing was a freak incident...It'll never happen again."

" Freak, hell. How many people were killed by the damned gulls? I used to think they were pretty, but now I'll go through life worrying about being attacked by them."

" Won't you even consider it? I mean, think about it."

" No," she demanded. "I don't have to think about a thing. I want out of here this afternoon, on the plane with the kids and back to Kansas, back to the corn fields, back to our home."

David was taken by the way that Marina would not even consider staying. He thought that he could at least get her to think about it.

" Well, I have to stay. At least to meet with Doug Porter and hear them out. If I turn this promotion down, I may not get another chance. They deserve my meeting with them."

" David," Marina interrupted. " This is our peace of mind we're talking about. We were happy in Kansas. This is just a vacation. The kids are happy in Kansas. Say no. It's not worth it. I would go out of my mind here. Every time I'd hear a gull, I would think about Erica and what happened. As it is, she's probably going to be scarred for life."

" Okay, Marina. You and the kids go back to Kansas. I'll stay and talk to them. Let me find out just how big the promotion is going to be. We can talk about it again before I decide."

" I can't believe you have to talk about it again," Marina continued. " This is our family. My God, David, this is our happy family we're talking about here. If you love me and the children, You'll say no to them."

" We better get you to the airport so you don't miss the plane."

" What about Chris?" Marina asked. " I understand they want him to appear on the morning show."

" No. I don't think it's a good idea. We've had enough of this thing. Byron can handle the news shows and setting the record straight about the whole thing."

Marina walked over to David and they embraced. The vacation was the farthest thing from enjoyable for them. David wanted to show Marina the best vacation on the island. But he felt that even through all that happened, they at least had each other.

GULLS

While they were standing there in the middle of the loft bedroom in a quiet embrace, Marina heard the click and then the sound of the motor as the curtains began to close. She flinched in his arms as the rollers pulled the white fabric toward the corner of the tall windows. The sudden reminder of the terror in the house with the captive gull caused Marina to reaffirm her belief that she had to return to Kansas.

Byron was waiting in the kitchen when Marina and David returned from upstairs.

"Well, Mr. and Mrs. Spencer. It's been nice. You've been more than nice. I hope to see you again."

"Next time you're in Kansas," Marina bid him.

"Right," Byron answered.

"Can I come back to visit?" Chris asked.

"This is my last summer here, Chris," Byron told him. "I go back to the west coast. As a matter of fact, next year I'm going to Vietnam."

"Where's Vietnam?" Chris asked.

"A long way from here, Chris. Well, I should be going. I have a lot to do to get ready for the New York thing."

Byron shook David's hand and gave Marina and Erica a hug. He turned to Chris and shook his small hand.

"Ma'am," he bid Kathleen as he started walking down the hall. Once outside, he paused for a second before getting into the Jeep. He stood looking at the Rutledge Place, thinking again of all that had taken place in the last days. Suddenly, the door opened. Chris appeared with his hands up to his face to shout.

" Hey, Byron, see ya ' ... wouldn't want to be ya '."

Byron returned a wide smile and jumped into the Jeep. He turned the wheel in the direction of the beach and quickly pushed the pedal causing the it to throw sand back and speed to the harder surface by the water. In the distance, he could see the many people lying in the sand and swimming in the ocean.

He passed by the many signs that said " **Do not feed the gulls.**" He knew that it wouldn't be long before the signs would be taken down and the gulls would return.

He arrived at the extreme north end of the island where the mountain of shells was piled. Parking a few hundred yards from the site, he watched as the gulls circled and dived at the hill of crustaceans. Again, he considered them as a thing of beauty. They flew in all directions and never touched wings. Like the great migrating birds from the north, they created a cloud of white as they enveloped the air above the hill. It wouldn't be long before he would leave this place. Next year, he would find himself in another land, far away from this small island. This was his life, he thought, studying these and other birds. As the hot air moved across the beach and brushed his face, he could smell the sea breeze and salt air. Suddenly, he heard the bulldozer's engine start as it began to push the mountain of shells. All would return to normal soon and the beaches would once again be theirs.

Back at the Rutledge Place, Marina and David packed the car with the luggage. Kathleen stood at the door as they bid their farewell to her. Soon they were on their way to the bridge that would take them off the island. As David drove the convertible across the bridge, a gull appeared again from out of nowhere. It flew along with them to the top of the arc of the bridge. Marina watched it with less fear than she had thought she could. Once again, she was able to look into its eye as it kept pace with them. There was a connection with the gull, Marina thought, an interaction. They all looked the same to her, yet each gull appeared a mystery. Were they, in fact, rats with wings? Or are they the romantic and graceful birds of summer? Remembering Erica and her lying in the sand, covered with blood, Marina felt they were truly rats with wings.

" Stop ! Stop!" Erica yelled to David.

As he pulled the car off to the shoulder of the road and came to a stop. Erica asked to get out.

" Can I feed them?" she asked.

" No! Don't be crazy. David, let's go," Marina demanded.

" It'll be all right, mother," Erica said.

" They won't hurt her, Marina," David told her.

Erica had Kathleen make some popcorn the night before and she had taken some with her. As she got out of the car and faced the bay, she threw a handful into the air. The wind took the corn and blew it toward the bridge. Taking a second handful and throwing it into the air, she watched as the first gull appeared.

kaaa, ka,ka,ka,kah,kah,ka it called out.

Soon, they came. And, like any other time at the beach, as done by millions of children and adults alike. They hovered close overhead as Erica threw some more to them.

" See, mother? They're fine. It was the lotion."

Marina got out of the car and considered throwing some morsels to them. She had second thoughts and watched as Erica threw the last of the corn into the air. Marina marveled at how resilient Erica was. She finally got to feed the gulls.

" C'mon Erica, We'll be late. We have to make the plane."

They headed past the hotels and on the ramp to the expressway toward Philadelphia. Soon the salt air left them and it was replaced by the hot and humid air of late summer.

Reflection

A few days later as the cool, almost cold air of Kansas continued to roll across the fields, Marina watched as the small birds did their acrobatic maneuvers. The phone rang. She went to the den and answered.

" Hello ? "she said softly.

" Hi, dear,"the voice on the other end of the line answered.

" David how are you?" she asked.

" Fine. Look, I'll be home soon, Marina."

" You will?" she asked. She could again hear the calmness in David's voice that she was used to.

" I've turned them down. Your right, we do have all we need in Kansas. We are happy there. Although the island is beautiful...Kansas is our home."

Marina couldn't control her tears as she listened to him. They were tears of joy.

"You and the kids are really what's important to me. If you're happy there then I'll be happy there. Like they say - If it ain't broke, don't fix it!"

After their short conversation, Marina turned

toward the sliding glass doors. She thought she was seeing things. Across the field, being chased by the small birds, was a gull. Marina watched as they chased and dived at it. Soon it was gone. She had no idea why the gull was so far inland or how it got here. All of a sudden it didn't matter to her. She knew one thing - if it returned she would have to tell the children...

Do not feed them.